Kenneth Frampton:
Conversations with Daniel Talesnik

Essay by Mary McLeod

Columbia Books on Architecture and the City

Contents

KENNETH FRAMPTON: CONVERSATIONS WITH DANIEL TALESNIK ESSAY BY MARY MCLEOD

COLUMBIA BOOKS ON ARCHITECTURE AND THE CITY

Kenneth Frampton's Idea of the "Critical"

Mary McLeod

Kenneth Frampton is arguably the most influential architectural historian since Sigfried Giedion. His book *Modern Architecture: A Critical History* has been released in five editions and translated into thirteen languages since it was first published in 1980, and his 1983 essay "Critical Regionalism: Six Points for an Architecture of Resistance" may have been translated into even more.[1] [Fig.1] Despite serious criticism about the essay's contradictions and limitations, including Frampton's own subsequent reservations about it,[2] it has probably had more impact on architects than any single essay published in the past fifty years—perhaps because of its ambiguities and contradictions.

Among the numerous architects who have cited this text as inspiration are John and Patricia Patkau (Patkau Architects) and Brigitte Shim and Howard Sutcliffe (Shim-Sutcliffe Architects) in Canada; Yvonne Farrell and Shelley McNamara (Grafton Architects) and Sheila O'Donnell and John Tuomey (O'Donnell + Tuomey) in Ireland; Wang Jun-Yang (Wang Jun-Yang Architects) in China; Rocco Yim (Rocco Design Architects) in Hong Kong; and Marina Tabassum

(Marina Tabassum Architects) in Bangladesh. [Figs. 2–3] While the writings of other architectural historians, such as Reyner Banham and Manfredo Tafuri, might have had a greater impact on scholars, Frampton's writings—a mixture of history, criticism, and analysis— have continued to inspire architects, especially those practicing outside of the United States (in places where the notion of "regionalism" or "locale" may have more resonance and meaning than in the States). Frampton's importance to architects might be compared to that of Vincent Scully, who gave credibility and support in the seventies and eighties to Louis Kahn, Robert Venturi, and the so-called "Grays"[3]—thus helping validate the rise of postmodern architecture in the United States. Or, if one looks to Europe, one might also compare Frampton to Paolo Portoghesi and Charles Jencks, who similarly encouraged the emergence of postmodernism during this period. However, Frampton's own influence on architects has been much broader and more enduring than that of these historians; it is genuinely global in its reach and has lasted more than fifty years. In describing his own role in architecture, Frampton modestly prefers the word "writer" to "historian," "theorist," or "critic."[4] But this choice of words might also reflect his refusal to draw sharp distinctions between these categories.[5] He freely admits to being engaged in "operative criticism," the practice that Tafuri so severely condemned in his 1968 book *Theories and History of Architecture*.[6]

Frampton was born in England in 1930 in the town of Woking, Surrey. He initially considered a career in agriculture but ultimately chose architecture, studying first at the Guildford School of Art and then in London at the Architectural Association (AA), where his teachers included Arthur Korn, Maxwell Fry and Jane Drew, and Alison and Peter Smithson. After graduating and working a few months at Chamberlin, Powell and Bon, Frampton spent two years in the British army (which he describes now as a complete waste of time), followed by one highly productive year working in Israel for the modernist architect Dov Karmi.[7] Returning to Britain in 1959, he spent a brief period at the Middlesex County Council, and then, from 1961 to 1965, was employed at Douglas Stephen & Partners in London, where he designed the Corringham housing complex (13–15 Craven Hill Gardens) in Bayswater, a project indebted both to Le Corbusier and to Soviet designers of the twenties. [Fig. 29 on pages 114–115] During this period, Frampton was further influenced by James Stirling's early architecture, especially his Leicester Engineering Building (which he considers a kind of synthesis of the work of Alvar Aalto and constructivism). While working at Stephen's office, Frampton wrote and co-edited his first book, *British Buildings 1960–1964*, and served, from 1962 to 1965, as technical editor of *Architectural Design* (*AD*). Inspired by Ernesto Rogers's journal, *Casabella continuità*, and Gae Aulenti's graphic design, he sought to give *AD* greater visual clarity and a more European outlook. He produced several notable issues on "local" architects—those working in a specific European cultural context, such as Gino Valle and Angelo Mangiarotti and Bruno Morassutti in Northern Italy.[8] [Fig. 4] Frampton would later describe Valle, who practiced almost exclusively in Udine, as a "critical regionalist" and subsequently as a representative of "tectonic culture," but at this stage the word "critical" was absent from his writings.[9]

In 1966, Frampton left England to accept a teaching position at Princeton University, where he remained until 1972 when he moved to Columbia University. For American architecture students in the late sixties and seventies, he was probably best known for his 1968 article in *AD* titled "The Humanist versus the Utilitarian Ideal," an analysis of Hannes Meyer's and Le Corbusier's entries for the 1927 League of Nations competition. [Figs. 37–38 on pages 143–144] Predictably, he sided with the humanist Le Corbusier, concluding that his project offered the possibility of both unifying and differentiating people in mass society.[10] It was this essay that led Robin Middleton, then the technical editor of *AD* and an acquisitions editor at Thames & Hudson, to ask Frampton to write a new survey of modern architecture. During this period, Frampton describes himself as "politically naïve" and not engaged with political theory other than with Hannah Arendt's *The Human Condition* (1958), which he read first in 1965 at the recommendation of Sam Stevens, a kind of polymath who taught architectural history in a "wildly sporadic fashion" at the AA.[11] (Arendt, who remains to this day a touchstone for Frampton's thought, is cited in "The Humanist versus the Utilitarian Ideal.") However, as just mentioned, in the early sixties Frampton was already interested in constructivism, although its fascination for him was more aesthetic than political, sparked by Camilla Gray's pioneering book of 1962, *The Great Experiment: Russian Art 1863–1922*. Not until 1968 would his political and aesthetic interests be conjoined; it was the year that he began writing about constructivist architecture, a subject largely missing from both Giedion's and Banham's surveys of modern architecture. By that time, Frampton was also a fellow at the New York–based Institute for Architecture and Urban Studies (IAUS), and in 1972, he would become one of the founding editors of its journal, *Oppositions*. [Fig. 5] That same year, he began teaching studio and history at Columbia University, where he continued to teach until 2021. Shortly thereafter, he designed his first and only realized building complex in the United States, Marcus Garvey Park Village housing in Brownsville, Brooklyn, sponsored by the IAUS. It was during these early years in the United States that Frampton first began to use the word "critical" to characterize his own writing and teaching.

Today, we take the word "critical" almost for granted as a term used to describe certain tendencies or ambitions in the writing of architectural history and in the design of certain kinds of architecture. Its usage has become almost ubiquitous, and it seems to serve as a trope indicating both analytical rigor and "leftist" political sympathies. [Fig. 6] During the past seventeen years or so, the word "critical" may have become better known in architecture circles for its countercurrent, the "postcritical," promoted by Robert Somol, Sarah Whiting, and Michael Speaks. Around 2002, these three young rebels reacted against certain poststructuralist currents in architecture, such as Derridean deconstruction and Lacanian analysis—that is, the arcane discourse that had dominated the journal *Assemblage* and so much of architectural theory in East Coast schools in the United States since the mid-eighties. In their view, theory had become too removed from the new parameters of practice—namely, digital technology and parametric design; just as significantly, it denied the sensuous experience of architecture.[12] Parenthetically, this use of the word "postcritical" in architecture is quite distinct (even if it overlaps in its appreciation of the sensuous) from the much earlier philosophical position first articulated by Michael Polanyi in the fifties and later elaborated on by William Poteat. These two thinkers sought a more encompassing form of knowledge, one that would go beyond conventional logic to embrace a personal knowledge of sense experience. In this regard, their position shared much with that of Maurice Merleau-Ponty and, indeed, of many of the figures whom Frampton himself admires, such as Arendt, despite their differing political perspectives.[13]

What is usually less recognized by architectural historians, theorists, and practitioners—whether pro- or post-critical—is how deeply indebted they are to Frampton for the term "critical" in architecture —and also, how distinct his own position is from the one rejected by Somol, Whiting, and Speaks (although undoubtedly, he would have some difficulties with their stance too). In 1980, Frampton was one of the first, if not the first, to use "critical" in the title of an English-language book on architecture (even though it should be stressed that he was, by no means, the first in architecture to be concerned with this issue—he was preceded by the earlier and more explicitly Marxist studies of the Venice School).[14] The word also appears in the titles of an *AD* publication that Frampton edited in 1982, *Modern Architecture and the Critical Present*, and of his influential 1983 essay "Towards a Critical Regionalism."[15] He employed it, too, in his teaching—in the title of the seminar "Comparative Critical Analysis of Built Form" that he taught at Princeton University beginning in the late sixties and then, intermittently, at Columbia University for almost fifty years. This pedagogical approach is encapsulated in his recent book, *A Genealogy of Modern Architecture: Comparative Critical Analysis of Built Form* (2015), which provides an eloquent synopsis of many of the concerns that have shaped Frampton's teaching over the years.[16]

13

But *what*, specifically, does Frampton mean by "critical"? Although he gives us a few hints as to its meaning, this is not something he has ever discussed at length. One might say the word is almost synecdochal for him in that it stands for a larger set of social concerns and agendas, including his commitment to leftist politics, which he has only occasionally articulated at length.[17]

The word "critical" has a long history, one that derives from the Greek word *kritikos*, meaning "judgment" or "discernment." Its modern usage derives first from Immanuel Kant's three *Critiques*, especially the *Critique of Pure Reason*, in which Kant attempts to examine the limits of the validity of a faculty, type, or body of knowledge through reflection; and second from Karl Marx's critique of political economy in *Capital*, in which critique is seen as a form of ideological dismantling, revealing the contradictions within capital itself. In general, this has meant that the word is associated with a certain kind of critical self-reflexivity (an examination that goes beyond intention or popular reception) and, in the case of Marxist theorists, a belief that such critical examination can contribute to social and political transformation. But Frampton's source, more specifically, like that for many others of his (and the subsequent) generation, is the Frankfurt School: the group of scholars who worked at the Institute for Social Research in the thirties, including Theodor Adorno, Max Horkheimer, and Herbert Marcuse, as well as others closely affiliated with it, such as Walter Benjamin. These scholars attempted to extend Marxism's ideological critique to the cultural sphere and to examine how mass culture had changed the production and reception of art—and thus its potential for radical social transformation. Critical Theory was intended to produce a type of knowledge—one grounded in the historical context of both the object of study and the researcher—that was both elucidating and emancipatory. In contrast to positivist knowledge (which envisions natural science as a model of all cognition), it was seen as a form of action or praxis, and thus a means for social betterment. This objective, too, is fundamental to Frampton's own work.

Frampton was among the first in the English-speaking architectural world to read and reflect upon the Frankfurt School and upon Benjamin's writings in particular. In his introduction to *Modern Architecture: A Critical History* (1980), he begins with a quote from Benjamin's "Theses on the Philosophy of History," and later admits that he was influenced by a Marxist interpretation of history, referring to his "affinity with the critical theory of the Frankfurt School," and the way that it made him "acutely aware of the dark side of the Enlightenment."[18] [Fig. 7]

Frampton's interest in Benjamin and the Frankfurt School, however, precedes the publication of *Modern Architecture* by more than a decade. In fact, he had already decided on the subtitle of the book in 1970 when he agreed to write the Thames & Hudson survey, and in 1972, he used the same passage from "Theses on the Philosophy of History" that opens *Modern Architecture* as an epigraph for his essay "Industrialization and the Crises in Architecture." This essay was published in the first issue of *Oppositions*, and he would later characterize the essay "as a somewhat naïve attempt to adopt a Benjaminian approach to historical phenomena."[19]

How did Frampton discover Benjamin and, more generally, leftist politics? Perhaps, not coincidentally, his seminal essay on Pierre Chareau's Maison de Verre appeared in the same 1969 issue of *Perspecta*, Yale's student-produced magazine, as Benjamin's synopsis of his *Arcades Project*, "Paris: Capital of the Nineteenth Century."[20] In some respects, this meticulously designed issue— its embossed cover evokes the rubber floor tiles of the Maison de Verre—encapsulates both sides of Frampton's thought: his deep concern for architecture's formal and structural qualities and his social and political investigations, through which he sought to establish the links between politics, social conditions, and form. [Fig. 40 on page 146] But more important, the sixties were a period of intense political engagement for many in the United States: first, the civil rights movement, followed by the increasingly intense protests against the Vietnam War, and then the women's liberation movement. Frampton has said that, paradoxically, it was coming to the States that "radicalized" him. He explains his conversion by quoting a comment that the English architect Michael Glickman once made to him: "You have to understand, in England the claws are hidden but in the States they are visible."[21] In other words, the brutality and pervasive power of capitalism and the military industrial state were blatantly apparent in the US. Like others at Princeton's School of Architecture, he was involved in the university strike in May 1970 after the Kent State massacre.

Frampton's interest in Benjamin was undoubtedly sparked by his admiration of Arendt (still very much apparent in his 2015 *Genealogy of Modern Architecture*). Arendt edited and wrote the introduction to *Illuminations*, the first collection in English of Benjamin's writings.[22] The book came out in 1968, and included Benjamin's best-known essay, "The Work of Art in the Age of Mechanical Reproduction," as well as his "Theses on the Philosophy of History." These two essays might be seen as embodying the two sides of Frampton's interest in Benjamin during this period: on the one hand, his almost utopian faith in technology's potential to improve human life and his deep commitment to mass housing, which parallels in some ways Benjamin's position in the first essay; and, on the other hand, his increasing pessimism about society's capacity to use technology judiciously and to sustain an authentic and meaningful culture in the face of ever-sweeping modernization, even as one accepts its inevitability—Paul Klee's angel being blown forward, even as he looks to the past, in Benjamin's "Theses." [Fig. 8]

16

An additional influence on Frampton in the late sixties was the work of the Frankfurt School philosopher Herbert Marcuse. Alan Colquhoun, who taught with Frampton at Princeton in the sixties, had given him his copy of *Eros and Civilization*, first published in 1955 and reissued in 1966.[23] In this book, which was seminal to the emergence of the New Left and a political strain of American counterculture, Marcuse focused not on class struggle but rather on the repression of eros, which he saw as the product of contemporary industrial relations, namely the alienated labor of "advanced industrial society." Marcuse called for a non-repressive civilization founded on non-alienated libidinal work, a goal reminiscent of that of the nineteenth-century French utopian socialist Charles Fourier. These themes resonated with Frampton's own growing concern for craft, an attention to detail—what one might call "care"—and for the sensuous aspects of architecture: or, to put it another way, his refusal to "separate the reality of work from the pleasure of life," as he so succinctly stated in his 1976 essay "The Volvo Case."[24] The role that Marcuse—and more generally the Frankfurt School—played in the evolution of Frampton's own thinking is most evident in the postscript to his 1983 essay on Arendt, "The Status of Man and the Status of His Objects." Here, he mentions two issues that he felt Arendt, who was not a Marxist, had either suppressed or suspended in her conclusion to *The Human Condition*: "First, the problematic cultural status of play and pleasure in a future labouring society after its hypothetical liberation from the compulsion of consumption (Marcuse) and, second, the remote and critical possibility for mediating the autonomous rationality of science and technique through the effective reconstitution of…an effective political realm (Habermas)."[25] Frampton's copy of *Eros and Civilization* is so well-worn and marked up that its cover and Colquhoun's inscription have long since disappeared. [Fig. 9]

Thus, it is these two authors—Benjamin and Marcuse—who introduced Frampton in the late sixties to the Frankfurt School and what came to be known as "Critical Theory." They would soon be followed by Jürgen Habermas, just cited, whose *Towards a Rational Society* (1967) was translated into English in 1970, and Adorno, whose *Minima Moralia* (1951) was translated into English in 1974.[26] Alessandra Latour, an Italian graduate student and teacher in urban design at Columbia (and then a committed Marxist), gave Frampton a copy of Adorno's book. His 1983 essay on Arendt begins with a quotation from it, one that again encapsulates the mixture of despair and messianic hope that has characterized so much of Frampton's own writing since the late sixties.[27] Until the eighties, very little by

17

Adorno or Horkheimer had been translated into English, and Frampton readily admits that he has never read from cover to cover the one book that seems to correspond most with his own disdain for commodification and mass culture: Adorno and Horkheimer's *Dialectic of the Enlightenment* (1947), translated into English in 1972.[28]

Two more thinkers, however—individuals with whom Frampton had direct personal contact—are also crucial to understanding his interest in Marxist cultural theory—especially concerning its potential application to architecture. The first is Tomás Maldonado, the Argentine painter, industrial designer, and theorist, who succeeded Max Bill as rector at the Hochschule für Gestaltung in Ulm and who was also a visiting professor at Princeton in the late sixties.[29] Frampton had already met Maldonado at Ulm in 1963, when he visited Germany as technical editor of *AD*;[30] at that time he encountered a second individual, the Swiss-French Marxist Claude Schnaidt, who also taught at Ulm and who would write the first monograph on Hannes Meyer, a book that Frampton has long admired.[31] Frampton discussed both writers in his 1974 essay, "Apropos Ulm: Curriculum and Critical Theory," in *Oppositions* 3, his first published use of the word "critical" in a title. In Ulm, he explained, he found a model for raising "critical consciousness of the role of design in contemporary society."[32] (Maldonado had, in fact, used "critical" in the subtitle of the 1972 English translation of *La Speranza Progettuale*, titled *Design, Nature, and Revolution: Toward a Critical Ecology*.) It should be noted, however, that Frampton's use of "critical" here has little to do with the Frankfurt School but rather with a more general commitment to a Marxist position that unites theory and action; in fact, Maldonado specifically cites Antonio Gramsci for his theory of "praxiology" or "theory of practice"—a "model of action oriented toward overcoming the dichotomy between theory and practice."[33] One of the most telling passages in *Modern Architecture: A Critical History* is from Schnaidt's essay, "Architecture and Political Commitment" of 1967. It is worth quoting in full, as it so eloquently summarizes the critical position that underlies Frampton's own text:

18

In the days when the pioneers of modern architecture were [still] young, they thought like William Morris that architecture should be an "art of the people for the people." Instead of pandering to the tastes of the privileged few, they wanted to satisfy the requirements of the community. They wanted to build dwellings, matched to human needs, to erect a Cité Radieuse. But they had reckoned without the commercial instincts of the bourgeoisie who lost no time in arrogating their theories to themselves and pressing them into service for the purposes of money-making. Utility quickly became synonymous with profitability. Anti-academic forms became the new décor of the ruling classes. The rational dwelling was transformed into the minimum dwelling, the Cité Radieuse into the urban conglomeration and austerity of line into poverty of form. The architects of the trade unions, co-operatives, and social municipalities were enlisted in the service of the whisky distillers, detergent manufacturers, the bankers, and the Vatican. Modern architecture, which wanted to play its part in the liberation of mankind by creating a new environment to live in, was transformed into a giant enterprise for the degradation of the human habitat.[34]

With this statement, Schnaidt (and thus Frampton) was insisting upon the need to recognize the extent to which modern architecture, despite its progressive intentions, had been shaped by the dictates of profit and capitalism. Also implicit in this passage, and perhaps even more clearly in Frampton's conclusion to the book, is their desire to propose something more than *Existenzminimum*— a commitment to a richer, more fulfilling world. And here, we have again the particular synthesis that underlies so much of Frampton's thought and what might be seen as the goal of his critical perspective: an architectural modernity that is not reduced to rational instrumentality and minimum dwelling, but rather offers a liberatory vision that enriches habitation and community life while still embracing technological progress. In other words, it is an architectural vision very much compatible with Marcuse's broader cultural argument in *Eros and Civilization*.

Frampton's discontent with architecture's commodification and environmental degradation was further fueled by the rise of postmodern architecture and its increasing emphasis on scenographic effects in design. This is very apparent by 1983, the year of his *AD* issue *Modern Architecture and the Critical Present* and the publication of "Towards a Critical Regionalism" in Hal Foster's anthology *The Anti-Aesthetic*. The anthology also included Habermas's sweeping indictment of postmodern thought, prompted by the Venice Architecture Biennale of 1980, and in part the motivation for Frampton's own essay (he was originally on the organizing committee of the Biennale but quickly resigned once he recognized the direction that Portoghesi's exhibition would take). [Fig. 13 on page 68] The intense debate among architects and social thinkers of the period arising from discussions about postmodernism had intensified Frampton's awareness not only of the failures and limits of the modern movement's embrace of technology and social transformation but also of the increasing complicity of contemporary architecture with the forces of capitalism. In other words, he used his citations of members of the Frankfurt School and Marxists such as Schnaidt and Maldonado to criticize both modern architecture and postmodern architecture, if increasingly with a critical lens directed at the latter. But it might also be said, as Fredric Jameson later so brilliantly explicated in *The Seeds of Time* (1994), that Frampton's "arrière-garde" critique was itself participating in the celebration of pluralism and difference so typical of both postmodernism and late capitalism (that is, a post-Fordist economy that can customize its products for local markets), even as it sought to retain some vestige of utopian hope in its proposal of an "architecture of resistance."[35] [Fig. 22 on page 92] One might say that Frampton hoped to fashion a progressive strategy out of

the materials of tradition and nostalgia (as well as a more considered use of technology) that would stand, even if metonymically,
against the commodification rampant in late capitalism.[36] He continued to share with Marcuse a belief in art as a reminder of an
alternative world, even as he acknowledged its incapacity to effect
large-scale change, at least without the presence of larger political, social, and cultural movements.

As important as the Frankfurt School was to Frampton, his understanding of what a critical position might entail can also be seen
as linked to another tradition, perhaps not consciously on his part,
one that has been fundamental to his thought since the early
seventies. Habermas, in his 1968 book *Knowledge and Human
Interests*, distinguished between critical political and social theory,
notably that of the Frankfurt School, and "self-reflective" cultural
theory. He equated the latter with hermeneutics, a theory concerned with the meaning of human texts and symbolic expressions,
one that effaces the boundary between factual and symbolic understanding.[37] While Habermas acknowledged the "conservative"
side of hermeneutics—that it is inherently concerned with existing
meanings and cultural tradition rather than with new possibilities,
and thus social transformation—he argued that it offers a necessary
critique of positivism in its insistence on individual life experience
which can then be adapted to general categories. Although literary
critical theory is now associated with numerous other tendencies,
including Derridean deconstruction, postcolonial theory, identity
politics, gender studies, and even environmental analyses, this
other—earlier—meaning of cultural theory articulated by Habermas
seems to reflect Frampton's own concerns for meaning and cultural expression (even if they have evolved over the years to include
some of the approaches just mentioned). This is perhaps most
apparent in his oft-cited and influential essay of 1983, "Towards a
Critical Regionalism," which opens with a long quotation from
Paul Ricoeur's 1961 essay "Universal Civilization and National Cultures." Ricoeur, known for uniting phenomenology and hermeneutics and for extending hermeneutic investigation beyond the literary

sphere, presciently posed the recurring quandary of developing nations (but one that affects all cultures): "There is the paradox: how to become modern and to return to sources: how to revive an old, dormant civilization"—which he referred to earlier as "a cultural past"—"and take part in universal civilization."[38] Frampton was introduced to Ricoeur's work by the phenomenologist Dalibor Vesely, who had opted not to review Frampton's *Modern Architecture* in the 1982 special issue of *AD*.[39]

Embracing Ricoeur's paradox—that is, between modernity and tradition or between universal civilization and regional cultures—Frampton proposed in "Towards a Critical Regionalism" a strategy of arrière-garde action, a kind of holding operation, salvaging the cultural meaning of architecture against the onslaught of an ever-pervasive instrumental rationality. The variety of sources in the essay is itself telling: not only his beloved Arendt, but also Marcuse, Benjamin, and Heidegger—in brief, both the Frankfurt School and phenomenology. In it, Frampton tries to find a means of practice that could unite his Marxist sympathies and deep commitment to an egalitarian society with his phenomenological or experiential concerns emphasizing place, light, and tactility—the sensuous dimensions of architecture (in fact, the very qualities that the postcritical crowd found missing in so much poststructuralist critical theory). While Frampton's effort to unite these two seemingly contradictory perspectives may be unique among architectural critics and historians—and distinct from Tafuri's position, let alone those of his IAUS colleagues—his struggle for such a synthesis was not so rare among philosophers, whether Marxists, such as Marcuse and Henri Lefebvre, or existentialists and phenomenologists, such as Jean-Paul Sartre and the younger Merleau-Ponty, who attempted to reconcile their philosophical ideas with their political commitment to a classless society (even if they would later part ways about the necessity of proletarian revolution). Tafuri himself admits in his largely positive review of Frampton's *Modern Architecture: A Critical History* that such a reconciliation between these two seemingly disparate positions is possible, although Frampton

22

himself has never tried systematically to do so in his writing.[40] Only later would he read seriously Merleau-Ponty's *Phenomenology of Perception* ([1945] 1962), a source that he cites in *A Genealogy of Modern Architecture*, in which the phenomenological strain in his thinking seems to dominate.

In "Towards a Critical Regionalism," one senses, perhaps more than in any of Frampton's other writings to date, the importance to him of the word "critical." He believed it was essential to distinguish his vision of regionalism from conservative appeals to nostalgia and tradition, and even from its lingering associations with the Nazi slogan "Blut und Boden"—a position he states forcefully in his third point.[41] Nonetheless, one wonders at times if his commitment to political critique is undermined or mitigated by his reveries about architecture's experiential qualities. Can the qualities that he so deeply values in architecture—such as tactility and the articulation of structure—really serve as modes of resistance, as a kind of arrière-garde holding operation? Is it possible to reconcile his belief in technology as a democratic and liberating tool that can improve living conditions for all classes, especially the most impoverished, with his rejection of mass culture and technology's pervasive presence in American society, which he associates with mindless gratification and environmental degradation (television, highways, air conditioning, and so on)? And given the proliferation of images and the homogenizing effects of ever-increasing globalization, is it possible to accept his preference for structure over surface effects, or his emphasis on place and urban identity, especially in contexts that do not possess any distinguishing regional or even topographical features? Like Lefebvre, who is not a central figure for Frampton but who also drew from both Marxism and phenomenology, Frampton seems to be searching for a logic (and in his case, an aesthetic vision) that can embrace the paradoxes of two seemingly disparate world views in his search for reservoirs of resistance against the onslaught of "commodity culture" and the "imperatives of production." And in a manner somewhat reminiscent of Benjamin, he relies on a series of quotations and fragments,

23

rather than one unified argument, to make his points.[42] But whether one accepts his synthesis or not, or even fully embraces his aesthetic vision, what undoubtedly makes his position so appealing to so many architects is his belief that critique should not be purely negative—that is, it should not only serve to elucidate the shortcomings and contradictions of the status quo but also take the risk of proposing alternatives that might offer, however modestly, the promise of a richer, more fulfilling existence.

If, over the years, Frampton has increasingly recognized the limits of architecture's own transformative powers given the hegemony of global capital, he still sees the proposing of positive examples of architecture as a "strategy of *sidestepping*—sidestepping a tendency toward closure that seems to constrain the living present in such a way that you sometimes feel you can't do anything."[43] Although these models reflect an increasing concern for the experiential qualities and what he calls the "poetics" of construction and structure, one thing has remained constant, as he recently stated: his "commitment to the socialist aspect of the modern project."[44] Here, his position seems closer to that of both Habermas and Gramsci, who emphasize culture's potential as a constructive force that can counter prevailing ideologies than to that of Tafuri and Adorno, who seem to accept a darker, more totalizing view of capitalism's power.[45] In fact, one might argue that where Frampton departs from Tafuri is not so much as an operative critic—for his models or preferences are not part of a seamless teleological narrative in the sense of Giedion or Bruno Zevi, two of Tafuri's "operative" historians—but rather in his willingness to propose strategies for architecture that might offer something more than the zero-sum game of market forces. To avoid closure, he seeks to present, as he has explained, a "wide variety of work."[46] [Figs. 10–12]

But the gap between Tafuri and Frampton might not be quite as great as it first appears. At the conclusion of *Architecture and Utopia*, and after a relentless account of modern architecture's "useless" utopianism and its serial failures to generate radical social change, Tafuri offers a glimmer of hope to architects: they might work in public offices as "technicians," that is, as organizers of building activities and planners of process, a role involving the dissolution of traditional disciplinary boundaries.[47] Frampton's hope, however, resides within architecture itself. He is still willing to see the generative—and positive—qualities of form and experience in order to create a space for an architectural practice that resists the most blatant forces of commodification.

Frampton is acutely aware of the difficulties of his own belief in the transformative values of both architecture and criticism, and in a 2001 interview with Gevork Hartoonian, he specifically addresses Tafuri's rejection of "operative history":

> I was recently re-reading the didactic introduction, wherein he [Tafuri] writes: "Doing away with outdated myths, one certainly does not see on the architectural horizon any ray of an alternative, of a technology 'of the working class.'" I am aware that the Marxist "hard line," then as now, thinks of my writing as operative criticism, as permitting the survival of anachronistic hopes of design as a liberative agent, which Tafuri dismissed as regressive. However, he also concedes that under present circumstances one is "left to navigate in empty space, in which anything can happen but nothing is decisive"— which sums up, I suppose, basically what I think about my position.[48]

In the last essay of his book *Labour, Work and Architecture*, "Minimal Moralia: Reflections on Recent Swiss German Production," a rather sharp assessment of some recent trends in Swiss architecture, Frampton states in a beautiful passage what navigating—and writing—in this "empty space" means to him:

One can only hope that others will be able to sustain their early capacity or, alternatively, to reveal an untapped potential for the pursuit of the art of architecture in all its anachronistic fullness. One perhaps needs to add that one does not indulge in critique for the sake of a gratuitous negativity, but rather to spur the critical sensibility, to sharpen the debate, to overcome, as far as this is feasible, the debilitating dictates of fashion, and above all to guard against the ever-present threat, in a mediatic age, of sliding into an intellectual somnambulance where everything seems to appear to be for the aestheticized best in the best of all commodified worlds.[49]

This essay, which was originally written for this publication, appeared with the same title in *Modern Architecture and the Lifeworld: Essays in Honor of Kenneth Frampton*, ed. Karla Cavarra Britton and Robert McCarter (London: Thames & Hudson, 2020), 20–42, published with the support of the Graham Foundation for Advanced Studies in the Fine Arts. I would like to acknowledge Tao Zhu, who first invited me to speak on this topic at Hong Kong University in a symposium, held in May 2016, in Kenneth Frampton's honor. An excerpt of this paper was also delivered at a workshop held at the Getty Research Institute, organized by Maristella Casciato and Gary Fox, in June 2019. I would like to express my gratitude to Cesare Birignani, Maristella Casciato, Meredith Clausen, Stephen Robert Frankel, Joe Hannan, and Joan Ockman, who all read earlier drafts of this essay.

1   Kenneth Frampton, *Modern Architecture: A Critical History* (London: Thames & Hudson, 1980; New York: Oxford University Press, 1980). Subsequent editions of *Modern Architecture* were published by Thames & Hudson in 1985, 1992, 2007, and 2020. The fifth edition significantly expands the book's geographical range. *Modern Architecture* has been translated into Chinese, Dutch, French, Estonian, German, Greek, Hungarian, Italian, Japanese, Portuguese, Russian, Serbian-Croatian, and Spanish. Kenneth Frampton, "Towards a Critical Regionalism: Six Points for an Architecture of Resistance," in *The Anti-Aesthetic: Essays on Postmodern Culture*, ed. Hal Foster (Port Townsend, WA: Bay Press, 1983), 16–30.

2   See especially, Kenneth Frampton, "Place-Form and Cultural Identity," in *Design After Modernism: Beyond the Object*, ed. John Thackara (London: Thames & Hudson, 1988), 51–66; and Kenneth Frampton, "Critical Regionalism Revisited," in *Critical Regionalism: The Pomona Proceedings*, ed. Spyros Amourgis (Pomona, CA: College of Environmental Design, California State Polytechnic University, 1991), 34–39. In "Place-Form and Cultural Identity," Frampton expresses reservations about the suffix "-ism" in his use of the word "regionalism" because of its links with style. Prior to the version of "Critical Regionalism" that appeared in the Foster anthology, Frampton wrote "Prospects for a Critical Regionalism" in 1982, which appeared in *Perspecta* 20 (1983), 177–195, and in 1985 he added in the second edition of *Modern Architecture* a concluding chapter, "Critical Regionalism: Modern Architecture and Cultural Identity," 313–327; in 1987, he wrote another essay "Ten Points on an Architecture of Regionalism: A Provisional Polemic," published in *Center 3: New Regionalism* (December 1987): 20–27. Although this essay does not have the word "critical" in the title, it concludes with a plea for a "critical

basis from which to evolve a contemporary architecture of resistance."

3   The "Grays" was a term used in the seventies to characterize a group of architects, including Romaldo Guirgola, Allan Greenberg, Charles Moore, Robert Venturi, and Robert A. M. Stern, who were seen as more "inclusive" in their approach to design—making references to vernacular forms and traditions—than the so-called "Whites," or the group of architects known as the "New York Five," who were influenced by Le Corbusier's modernist villas of the twenties.

4   Kenneth Frampton, preface to Labour, Work and Architecture: Collected Essays on Architecture and Design (London: Phaidon, 2002), 6; see also Kenneth Frampton and Daniel Talesnik's conversation on October 22, 2013, on page 171 of this volume.

5   I am indebted to Cesare Birignani, who read an earlier version of this paper, for this observation.

6   Frampton, preface to Labour, Work and Architecture, 7; Manfredo Tafuri, Theories and History of Modern Architecture, trans. Giorgio Verrecchia (New York: Harper & Row, 1980), 141–170. In this book, first published in Italian in 1968, Tafuri defined "operative criticism" as "an analysis of architecture (or the arts in general) that, instead of an abstract survey, has as its objective the planning of a precise poetical tendency, anticipated in its structures and derived from historical analyses programmatically distorted and finalised" (page 141).

7   Kenneth Frampton, conversation with the author, May 21, 2018; he also talked about this period in his conversation with Daniel Talesnik on June 26, 2012, on page 95 of this volume.

8   Kenneth Frampton, ed., "Italy. The Work of Mangiarotti & Morassutt & Gino Valle," Architectural Design 34, no. 3 (March 1964).

9   At AD, he also published Constant Nieuwenhuys's "New Babylon: An Urbanism of the Future," Architectural Design 34, no. 6 (June 1964): 304–305; as well as Yona Friedman's "Ports on Channel Bridge," Architectural Design 33 (April 1963): 158–159; and his "Towards a Mobile Architecture," Architectural Design 33 (November 1963): 509–510.

10   Kenneth Frampton, "The Humanist versus the Utilitarian Ideal," Architectural Design 38, no. 3 (March 1968): 134–136, repr. in Frampton, Labour, Work and Architecture, 109–119. In a 2003 interview with Stan Allen and Hal Foster, Frampton explained his preference for Le Corbusier over Meyer in a query about Michael Hays's more positive assessment of Meyer. "Your question makes me think again of the limits of any particular historical moment. Is it unfair to suggest that the critical rigor upheld by Hays and possibly by Tafuri, in their defense of the anticompositional and the antihumanist, is still a form of waiting, as it were, for the revolutionary moment when a radical transformation might occur and a new acceptance of the fact that this is hardly likely to happen, that this

option might not be available anymore. Then the question arises: which is the more realist of the two positions? It's not that I'm against what Hannes Meyer represented, but on a broader historical front, I have to ask which position is the more operatively critical." Stan Allen and Hal Foster, "A Conversation with Kenneth Frampton," *October* 106 (Autumn 2003): 56.

11   Frampton, conversation with the author, May 21, 2018.

12   See Robert Somol and Sarah Whiting, "Notes around the Doppler Effect and Other Moods of Modernism," *Perspecta* 33, "Mining Autonomy" (2002): 72–77; and Michael Speaks, "Design Intelligence and the New Economy," *Architectural Record* 190, no. 1 (January 2002): 72–79.

13   Michael Polanyi, *Personal Knowledge: Towards a Post-Critical Philosophy* (Chicago: University of Chicago Press, 1958); William H. Poteat, *Polanyian Meditations: In Search of a Post-Critical Logic* (Durham, NC: Duke University Press, 1985).

14   Here, it is important to acknowledge Manfredo Tafuri's *Theories and History of Architecture* of 1968, in which he explored issues of historiography and criticism in depth, drawing heavily from the work of the Frankfurt School, especially the writings of Walter Benjamin. In the introduction to his book *The Sphere and the Labyrinth*, Tafuri quoted at length from Giulio Carlo Argan's *La crisi dei valori* (1957), which he credited as a source for his own ideas about a more "advanced" criticism. *The Sphere and the Labyrinth: Avant-Gardes and Architecture from Piranesi to the 1970s,* trans. Pellegrino d'Acierno and Robert Connolly (Cambridge, MA: MIT Press, 1987), 7. As is noted later in this essay, the only previous use of the word "critical" that I have found in the title of an English-language architecture book is Tomás Maldonado, *Design, Nature, Revolution: Toward a Critical Ecology,* trans. Mario Domandi (New York: Harper and Row, 1972), the English translation of *La Speranza Progettuale* (Turin: G. Einaudi, 1970); note that the word does not appear in the original Italian title.

15   Kenneth Frampton, ed., *Modern Architecture and the Critical Present* (London: Architectural Design Profile, 1982).

16   Kenneth Frampton, *A Genealogy of Modern Architecture: Comparative Critical Analysis of Built Form*, ed. Ashley Simone (Zurich: Lars Müller, 2015).

17   My observations are based in part on having known Frampton over the past forty years (including several conversations with him about his interest in the Frankfurt School) and in part on writings and published interviews. Kenneth Frampton, telephone conversation with the author, May 16, 2016; Frampton, conversation with the author, May 21, 2018. See also Gevork Hartoonian, "An Interview with Kenneth Frampton," January 2001, *Architectural Theory Review* 7, no. 1 (2002), repr. *Global Perspectives on Critical Architecture: Praxis*

Reloaded, ed. Hartoonian (Farnham, Surrey: Ashgate, 2015), 43–47; Allen and Foster, "A Conversation with Kenneth Frampton"; and Monika Mitásová, "Kenneth Frampton," January 19 and 25, 2010, in *Oxymoron & Pleonasm: Conversations on American Critical and Projective Theory of Architecture*, ed. Monika Mitásová (New York: Actar, 2014), 10–28. I have also drawn from the interviews by Daniel Talesnik in this book (See note 1).

18   Kenneth Frampton, introduction to *Modern Architecture: A Critical History* (New York and Toronto: Oxford University Press, 1980), 8–9. This introduction is included in all subsequent editions.

19   Allen and Foster, "A Conversation with Kenneth Frampton," 42; Frampton's essay "Industrialization and the Crises in Architecture" (*Oppositions* 1 [1973]: 53–81) was written for a conference in honor of Hannah Arendt, which she attended.

20   Kenneth Frampton, "Maison de Verre," and Walter Benjamin, "Paris: Capital of the Nineteenth Century," *Perspecta* 12 (1969): 77–125 and 161–172. Both articles played a seminal role in introducing new material to English-speaking architects and, more generally, to American readers. *Perspecta* republished the recent translation of "Paris, Capital of the Nineteenth Century" by Quintin Hoare, which had appeared in *New Left Review* 48 (March–April 1968): 77–88, adding illustrations by Grandville to accompany the text. *Perspecta* also included Ben Brewster's introduction to Benjamin's synopsis, "Walter Benjamin and the Arcades Project," which had also first been published in the same issue of *New Left Review*. It would not be until 1978 that the synopsis would be published in the anthology of Walter Benjamin's writings *Reflections*, ed. Peter Demetz, trans. Edmund Jephcott (New York: Harcourt Brace Jovanovich, 1978).

21   Frampton, phone conversation with the author, May 16, 2016.

22   Walter Benjamin, *Illuminations*, trans. Harry Zohn (New York: Schocken Books, 1968).

23   See Herbert Marcuse, *Eros and Civilization* (Boston: Beacon Press, 1955). Tomás Maldonado, who also taught at Princeton in the late sixties, was probably responsible for alerting both Frampton and Colquhoun to Marcuse. In his interview with Allen and Foster, Frampton speculates that being in the United States also "politicized" Colquhoun and precipitated his turn toward Marxism (page 41).

24   Kenneth Frampton, "The Volvo Case," *Lotus*, no. 12 (1976), repr. in Frampton, *Labour, Work and Architecture*, 64–75. Frampton had already used a passage from *Eros and Civilization* (New York: Vintage Books, 1962), 139 as an epigraph to his article "The City of Dialectic," published in *Architectural Design* 39, no. 10 (October 1969): 541, and he referred to the same passage from *Eros and Civilization* in his essay "America 1960–1970: Appunti su alcune immagini e teorie della città," "America 1960–1970: Notes on Urban Images

and Theory, *Casabella* 35, no. 359–360 (December 1971): 34, 36.

25   Kenneth Frampton, "The Status of Man and the Status of His Objects: A Reading of *The Human Condition*," in *Modern Architecture and the Critical Present*, 15, repr. in Frampton, *Labour, Work and Architecture*, 39.

26   In his essay "Place-Form and Cultural Identity," Frampton refers to Jürgen Habermas's essay "Technology and Science as Ideology" in *Towards a Rational Society* as "a seminal work" and states that "the later Frankfurt School remains," in his view, "the only valid basis upon which to develop a form of (post) modern critical culture." Frampton, "Place-Form and Cultural Identity," in *Design After Modernism*, 63.

27   "The only philosophy which can be responsibly practiced in the face of despair is the attempt to contemplate all things as they would present themselves from the standpoint of redemption; all else is reconstruction, mere technique. Perspectives must be fashioned that displace and estrange the world, reveal it to be, with its rifts and crevices, as indigent and distorted as it will appear one day in the messianic light." Theodor Adorno, *Minima Moralia* (1947), quoted in Frampton, *Labour, Work and Architecture*, 25.

28   Over the years Frampton has frequently expressed his sympathy for Clement Greenberg's argument in his 1939 essay "Avant-Garde and Kitsch." One of his most explicit rejections of mass culture and popular taste occurs in his vehement exchange with Denise Scott Brown in the December 1971 issue of *Casabella*. Frampton, "America 1960–1970: Notes on Urban Image and Theory," and Denise Scott Brown, "Pop Off: Reply to Kenneth Frampton," *Casabella*, no. 359–360 (December 1971): 24–38 and 41–45. Besides *New Left Review* (the source of *Perspecta*'s translation of Walter Benjamin's "Paris: Capital of the Nineteenth-Century"), a major source of translations of writings by the Frankfurt School and related theorists such as Siegfried Kracauer was the journal *New German Critique*, founded in 1973. Adorno's *Aesthetic Theory* (published posthumously in 1970) was not translated until 1984.

29   It was a young, precocious Argentine student at Princeton at the time, Emilio Ambasz, who was probably responsible for encouraging Dean Robert Geddes to bring Maldonado to Princeton to teach. Ambasz remains an important supporter of Frampton's research.

30   Monica Pidgeon, the editor of *AD*, accompanied Kenneth Frampton on this trip.

31   Claude Schnaidt, *Hannes Meyer: Buildings, Projects and Writings* (Teufen, CH: Arthur Niggli, 1965).

32   Kenneth Frampton, "Apropos Ulm: Curriculum and Critical Theory," *Oppositions* 3 (1974):17. The essay, but not the introduction from which this quotation is taken, is reprinted in *Labour, Work and Architecture*, 45–63.

33   Tomás Maldonado, "Colloquium con Maldonado e Ohl," *Design-*

Italia 3 (September 1972): 32, quoted in Frampton, "Apropos Ulm: Curriculum and Critical Theory," 34. Maldonado was also influenced by the Marxist philosopher Ernst Bloch, and the word "speranza" in his book title *La Speranza Progettuale* (The Principle of Hope) alludes to Bloch's *Das Prinzip Hoffnung*, which Maldonado cites extensively. See Maldonado, *Design, Nature, and Revolution: Toward a Critical Ecology*, trans. Mario Domandi (Minneapolis: University of Minnesota Press, 2019).

34   Claude Schnaidt, "Architektur und politisches Engagement" [Architecture and Political Commitment], *Ulm*, no. 19/20 (August 1967): 26, quoted in Frampton, *Modern Architecture*, 285–286. The passage is the opening paragraph of a talk that Schnaidt gave at the Academy of Fine Arts in Hamburg on March 2, 1967.

35   Fredric Jameson, *The Seeds of Time* (New York: Columbia University Press, 1994), 188–205.

36   Jameson, *The Seeds of Time*, 202–204.

37   Jürgen Habermas, *Knowledge and Human Interests*, trans. Jeremy J. Shapiro (Boston: Beacon Press, 1971). The original German book was published in 1968. Frampton told me that he has not read it.

38   Paul Ricoeur, "Universal Civilization and National Culture" (1961), in *History and Truth*, trans. Charles A. Kelbley (Evanston, IL: Northwestern University Press, 1965), 276–277, quoted in Frampton, "Towards a Critical Regionalism," 16.

39   Frampton dedicates *A Genealogy of Modern Architecture* to Vesely.

40   Manfredo Tafuri, "Architecture and 'Poverty,'" in *Modern Architecture and the Critical Present*, 57–58. Tafuri wrote: "It is hardly accidental that Frampton's critical sensibility enters into tension with the ethos that he has himself inherited from the 'tradition of the new.' Benjamin and Heidegger, in truth, are not irreconcilable. Yet still, a work of historical reconstruction is needed in order to open up a dialogue between them, the kind of work that hasty readers of Lyotard would barely be able to handle" (page 58). Tafuri seems to imply that Frampton in "his excellent book" should have "cleansed" modern architecture even more, and stated more forcefully the need for "destruction" and poverty" as a precondition for new "paths." In his review, Tafuri cites Benjamin's essay "The Destructive Character" (1931), which had not yet been translated into English. His title and argument also suggest Benjamin's essay "Experience and Poverty" (1932), which had also not yet been translated into English. Tafuri's willingness to consider a reconciliation between Marxism and phenomenology was undoubtedly spurred by the work of Massimo Cacciari, who taught aesthetics at the University of Venice and was deeply influenced by Nietzsche and Heidegger.

41   Frampton, "Towards a Critical Regionalism," 20.

42   In the case of Frampton's essay, the choice to structure the es-

say as a series of points is also reminiscent of modernist manifestos such as Le Corbusier and Pierre Jeanneret's "Five Points of a New Architecture" (1926). Frampton's use of "Towards" also recalls—and was undoubtedly meant to evoke— the English title of Le Corbusier's *Vers une architecture* (1923), translated into English in 1927 as *Towards a New Architecture*.

43   Allen and Foster, "A Conversation with Kenneth Frampton," 57.

44   See Kenneth Frampton and Daniel Talesnik's conversation on October 22, 2013, on page 171 of this volume.

45   In the "Note to the Second Edition" of *Theories and History of Architecture* (n.p.), Tafuri dismisses all "sugary official 'Marxism,'" including the Marcusian school, and rejects the notion of a "class architecture (an architecture 'for a liberated society')," arguing that it results in an ideology that only serves the status quo.

46   Allen and Foster, "A Conversation with Kenneth Frampton, 57.

47   Manfredo Tafuri, *Architecture and Utopia: Design and Capitalist Development*, trans. Barbara Luigia La Penta (Cambridge, MA: MIT Press, 1976), 170–182.

48   Frampton, in "Interviewed by Gevork Hartoonian," in *Global Perspectives on Critical Architecture*, 46. Frampton follows this passage by declaring, "I fail to see how my discourse preoccupied with regionalism and tectonics can be seen as perpetuating illusions as to the 'utopia of design,' to coin Tafuri's phrase."

49   Frampton, "Minimal Moralia: Reflections on Recent Swiss German Production" (1997), in *Labour, Work and Architecture*, 331.

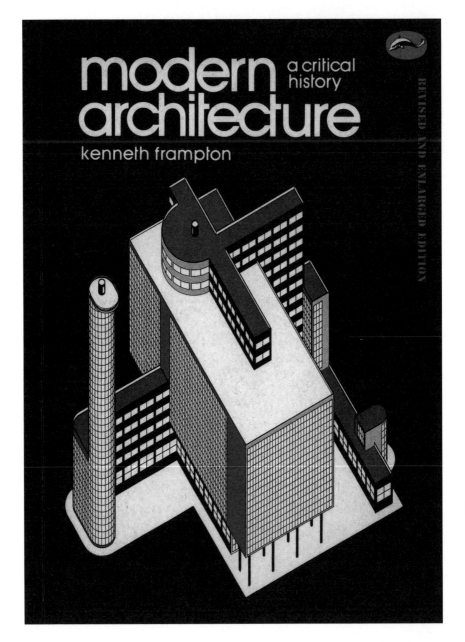

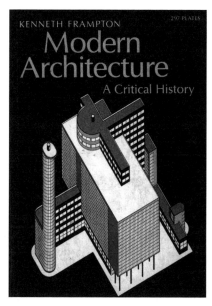

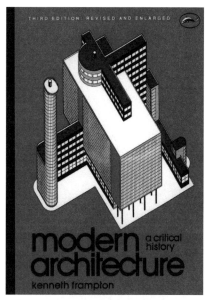

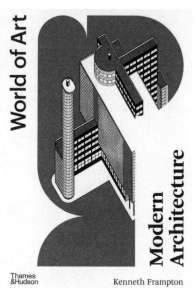

Fig. 2   Marina Tabassum, Bait Ur Rouf Mosque, Dhaka, Bangladesh, 2012. Photograph by Rajesh Vora. ©Aga Khan
Trust for Culture/Rajesh Vora. Kenneth Frampton invited Tabassum to give the ninth annual Kenneth
Frampton Endowed Lecture at Columbia University's Graduate School of Architecture, Planning, and Pres-
ervation, September 2019.

39

Fig. 4   Cover of Kenneth Frampton, ed., "Italy/The Work of Mangiarotti & Morassutti & Gino Valle,"
         Architectural Design 34, no. 3 (March 1964).

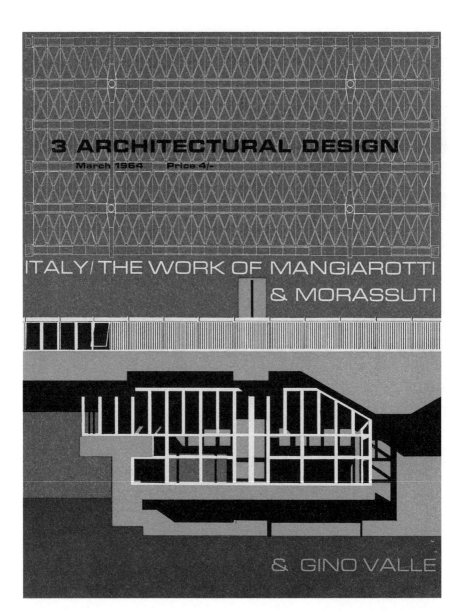

Fig. 5   Cover of Kenneth Frampton, ed., "Le Corbusier: 1933–1960," special issue, *Oppositions* 19/20 (Winter/Spring 1980).

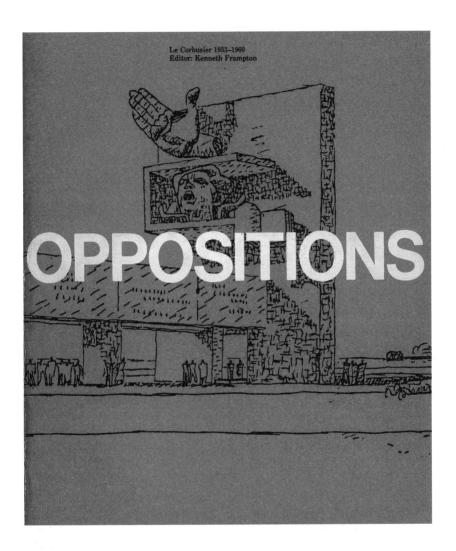

Fig. 6   Some books on architecture, following Frampton's *Modern Architecture: A Critical History*, with the
         word "critical" in their titles. Below: Marc Treib, *Modern Landscape Architecture: A Critical Review*
         (Cambridge, MA: MIT Press, 1993). Opposite page: Jane Rendell, Jonathan Hill, Murray Fraser, and
         Mark Dorrian, *Critical Architecture* (London: Routledge, 2007); Elie G. Haddad and David Rifkind, ed.,
         A Critical History of Contemporary Architecture, 1960–2010 (Surrey: Ashgate, 2014); Thorsten Botz-
         Bornstein, *Transcultural Architecture: The Limits and Opportunities of Critical Regionalism* (Surrey:
         Ashgate, 2015); and Gevork Hartoonian, ed., *Global Perspectives on Critical Architecture: Praxis
         Reloaded* (Surrey: Ashgate, 2015).

42

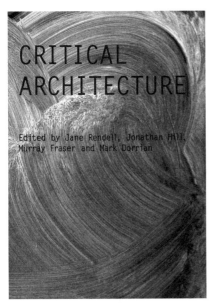

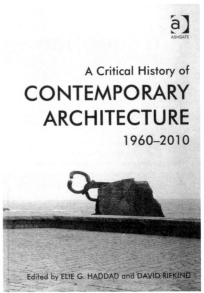

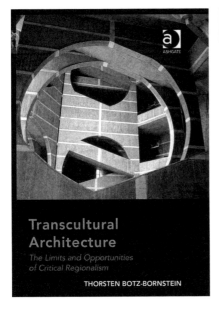

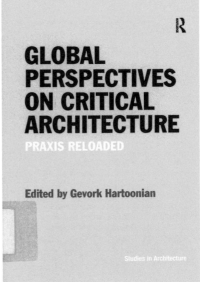

Introduction

A Klee painting named 'Angelus Novus' shows an angel looking as though he is about to move away from something he is fixedly contemplating. His eyes are staring, his mouth is open, his wings are spread. This is how one pictures the angel of history. His face is turned towards the past. Where we perceive a chain of events, he sees one single catastrophe which keeps piling wreckage upon wreckage and hurls it in front of his feet. The angel would like to stay, awaken the dead, and make whole what has been smashed. But a storm is blowing from Paradise; it has got caught in his wings with such violence that the angel can no longer close them. This storm irresistibly propels him into the future to which his back is turned, while the pile of debris before him grows skyward. This storm is what we call progress.

Walter Benjamin
Theses on the Philosophy of History
1940

One of the first tasks to be faced in attempting to write a history of modern architecture is to establish the beginning of the period. The more rigorously one searches for the origin of modernity, however, the further back it seems to lie. One tends to project it back, if not to the Renaissance, then to that moment in the mid-18th century when a new view of history brought architects to question the Classical canons of Vitruvius and to document the remains of the antique world in order to establish a more objective basis on which to work. This, together with the extraordinary technical changes that followed throughout the century, suggests that the necessary conditions for modern architecture appeared some time between the physician–architect Claude Perrault's late 17th-century challenge to the universal validity of Vitruvian proportions and the definitive split between engineering and architecture which is sometimes dated to the foundation in Paris of the Ecole des Ponts et Chaussées, the first engineering school, in 1747.

Here it has been possible to give only the barest outline of this prehistory of the Modern Movement. The first three chapters, therefore, are to be read in a different light from the rest of the book. They treat of the cultural, territorial and technical transformations from which modern architecture emerged, offering short accounts of architecture, urban development and engineering as these fields evolved between 1750 and 1939.

The critical issues to be broached in writing a comprehensive but concise history are first, to decide what material should be included, and second, to maintain some kind of consistency in the interpretation of the facts. I have to admit that on both counts I have not been as consistent as I would have wished; partly because information often had to take priority over interpretation, partly because not all the material has been studied to the same degree of depth, and partly because my interpretative stance has varied according to the subject under consideration. In some instances I have tried to show how a particular approach derives from socio-economic or ideological circumstances, while in others I have restricted myself to formal analysis. This variation is reflected in the structure of the book itself, which is divided into a mosaic of fairly short chapters that deal

8

44

Fig. 8   Paul Klee, *Angelus Novus*, 1920. Photograph by Elie Posner. ©The Israel Museum, Jerusalem. Walter
          Benjamin bought this oil-transfer drawing in 1921 and it hung in every apartment in which he lived.

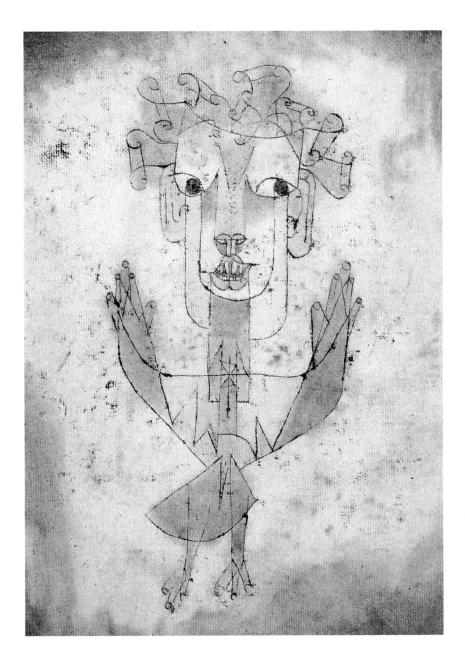

45

138   EROS AND CIVILIZATION

distribution of scarcity (as may, for example, have existed in matriarchal phases of ancient society). The second would pertain to a rational organization of fully developed industrial society after the conquest of scarcity. The vicissitudes of the instincts would of course be very different under these two conditions, but one decisive feature must be common to both: the instinctual development would be non-repressive in the sense that at least the surplus-repression necessitated by the interests of domination would not be imposed upon the instincts. This quality would reflect the prevalent satisfaction of the basic human needs (most primitive at the first, vastly extended and refined at the second stage), sexual as well as social: food, housing, clothing, leisure. This satisfaction would be (and this is the important point) *without toil*—that is, without the rule of alienated labor over the human existence. Under primitive conditions, alienation has *not yet* arisen because of the primitive character of the needs themselves, the rudimentary (personal or sexual) character of the division of labor, and the absence of an institutionalized hierarchical specialization of functions. Under the "ideal" conditions of mature industrial civilization, alienation would be completed by general automatization of labor, reduction of labor time to a minimum, and exchangeability of functions.

Since the length of the working day is itself one of the principal repressive factors imposed upon the pleasure principle by the reality principle, the reduction of the working day to a point where the mere quantum of labor time no longer arrests human development is the first prerequisite for freedom. Such reduction by itself would almost certainly mean a considerable decrease in the standard of living prevalent today in the most advanced industrial countries. But the regression to a lower standard of living, which the collapse of the

Regression to a lower standard of living related to FREEDOM

performance principle would bring about, does not militate against progress in freedom.

The argument that makes liberation conditional upon an ever higher standard of living all too easily serves to justify the perpetuation of repression. The definition of the standard of living in terms of automobiles, television sets, airplanes, and tractors is that of the performance principle itself. Beyond the rule of this principle, the level of living would be measured by other criteria: the universal gratification of the basic human needs, and the freedom from guilt and fear—internalized as well as external, instinctual as well as "rational." "La vraie civilization . . . n'est pas dans le gaz, ni dans la vapeur, ni dans les tables tournantes. Elle est dans la diminution des traces du péché originel" [17]—this is the definition of progress beyond the rule of the performance principle.

Under optimum conditions, the prevalence, in mature civilization, of material and intellectual wealth would be such as to allow painless gratification of needs, while domination would no longer systematically forestall such gratification. In this case, the quantum of instinctual energy still to be diverted into necessary labor (in turn completely mechanized and rationalized) would be so small that a large area of repressive constraints and modifications, no longer sustained by external forces, would collapse. Consequently, the antagonistic relation between pleasure principle and reality principle would be altered in favor of the former. Eros, the life instincts, would be released to an unprecedented degree.

Does it follow that civilization would explode and revert to prehistoric savagery, that the individuals would die as a result of the exhaustion of the available means

47

[17] "True civilization does not lie in gas, nor in steam, nor in turntables. It lies in the reduction of the traces of original sin." Baudelaire, *Mon Coeur Mis à Nu*, XXXII, in *Oeuvres Posthumes*, ed. Conard, Vol. II (Paris, 1952), p. 109.

Fig. 10   Alvar Aalto, Säynätsalo Town Hall, Säynätsalo, Finland, 1949–1951. Photograph by Marc Treib.

49

51

Conversations
Kenneth Frampton and Daniel Talesnik

Note to Readers

This book is both a history and a personal reflection on the work of one of architecture's most enduring writers. These interviews open a window onto a relational way of thinking about architecture, one in which buildings and architects are always understood in reference to other cultural patterns. They unfold a thought process where Frampton is constantly editing, refining, and reacting to his own work, a practice that is continued over the course of these conversations.

The seven interviews that follow span Frampton's early days as an architecture student at the Guildford School of Art to his decades-long tenure as a professor at Columbia University. Together, they capture the circumstances—personal, political, social, cultural— in which he started writing, thinking, and publishing his ideas on architecture, providing a framework not only for his time as technical editor of *Architectural Design* but also for some of his most resounding publications. In sketching out the intellectual atmosphere of architectural culture on both sides of the Atlantic from the sixties onward, the conversations also reveal how this theoretical terrain informed his most critical contributions to architectural thought and practice.

This project began during my time as a PhD candidate at Columbia University. I received support for the project from the university's Temple Hoyne Buell Center for the Study of American Architecture, and we held the first two conversations in the fall of 2011 as part of an Oral History seminar. We continued these conversations, following the arc of Frampton's professional and personal biography, over the course of two years, and this led to deeper ruminations on built and written forms of architectural production. This collection of interviews meanders, producing not a straightforward account but an entangled discursive map of his life and ideas. Together they reveal a portrait that is as much about Frampton himself as about the cultural environment from which his work emerged.

Daniel Talesnik
Munich, December 2019

October 4, 2011

D   T   Daniel Talesnik
K   F   Kenneth Frampton

D T Despite both the great volume and impact of your written work—*Modern Architecture: A Critical History* will soon have five editions which proves its success as a pedagogical textbook around the world—you are perhaps best known for your idea of "critical regionalism."[1] What was the context that drove you to this idea?

K F This relates to a moment at Columbia University's School of Architecture when Robert Stern was on the faculty and had a lot of influence, a moment when the postmodern style emerged at the school. In 1979, Stern invited me to participate as a commissioner in the planning of the 1980 Venice Architecture Biennale organized by Paolo Portoghesi, which was staged under the slogan: "The Presence of the Past." [Fig.13] I went to Venice for the first meeting and afterwards I resigned. I sensed the demagogic nature of the whole operation, which included the installation of the Strada Novissima in the Arsenale, lined with scenographic façades by different architects. [Fig.14] When I came back, I felt that the idea of modernity with which I had been educated as a student was no longer viable. On the other hand, I felt that the emerging postmodernist style was mostly a gratuitous and kitsch reaction to the ideological crisis in architecture at the time.

It so happened that this Venice Biennale coincided with the first publication of *Modern Architecture: A Critical History*. Andreas Papadakis, who was then the owner and editor of *Architectural Design*, persuaded Thames & Hudson to let him publish extracts from the book in a special issue of the magazine, which eventually appeared under the title *Modern Architecture and the Critical Present*.[2] This gave me the opportunity to invite certain figures to write reviews of the book and various architects and intellectuals participated, including Alan Colquhoun, Rafael Moneo, and Manfredo Tafuri. I also invited the late Czech émigré and architect/philosopher Dalibor Vesely, who was teaching at Cambridge University. Dalibor declined to write but he instead advised me that what I explored in the last chapter of the book had been reflected upon by Paul Ricoeur in his 1963 essay "Universal Civilization and National Cultures."[3] I duly read this essay and I was immediately enlightened

61

by the precise and profound distinction Ricoeur drew between universal civilization and national cultures.

In 1981, Alexander Tsonis and Liliane Lefaivre published an essay in the magazine *Architecture in Greece* titled "The Grid and the Pathway."[4] [Fig. 15] It was, in effect, a critique of the work of two prominent Greek architects, Dimitris Pikionis and Aris Konstantinidis. "Pathway" referred to the architecture of Pikionis, while "grid" referred to the architecture of Konstandinidis. In using these terms, they articulated the opposition between the topographic emphasis of Pikionis, and the more "rational" orthogonal dimension of Konstandinidis. It was Tsonis and Lefaivre who coined the term "critical regionalism." I was very inspired by it, and I used it in my essay "Towards a Critical Regionalism, Six Points for an Architecture of Resistance," which I wrote for a compilation of essays edited by Hal Foster titled *The Anti-Aesthetic: Essays on Postmodern Culture* in 1983.[5]

D T Some of the architects whose work you analyzed in illustrating the idea of critical regionalism moved on to work internationally: Álvaro Siza designed buildings in Germany and the Netherlands. He, more recently, designed the Fundação Iberê Camargo in Brazil. Tadao Ando often worked outside of Japan from the millennium on. In a sense, critical regionalism went "on the road."

K F For a talk in Dublin at the Royal Institute of the Architects of Ireland, I was asked to address the question of critical regionalism as a general world condition. The president of the institute had remarked that, given Ireland's current state of economic depression, Irish architects would probably have to work outside the country and wondered where they stood in regards to regionalism. What is interesting about the current situation is the way in which somebody from a particular region is able to work in another country in a manner that is particularly sensitive to the native culture. Siza's Iberê Camargo museum in Porto Alegre, executed in reinforced concrete, is a case in point for the way it alludes to the Brazilian concrete tradition. [Fig. 16] In fact, I believe there are not many exposed reinforced concrete buildings by Siza and, in this regard, the building is significant. This is an example of an architect from outside a country responding in a particularly sensitive way to the local tradition. This intervention reminds me of the Brazilian architect Lúcio Costa, who went from Brazil to Portugal looking for the roots of the Portuguese vernacular while taking with him his own knowledge of the Brazilian vernacular. Costa's visit had a strange effect on the Portuguese, provoking Carlos Ramos—the director of the school of architecture in Porto during the Salazar period—to initiate a state-sponsored research program on Portuguese vernacular architecture. Many architects, including Siza, Fernando Tavora, and others from all over the country, became part of a countrywide effort to photograph and measure examples of the Portuguese vernacular, eventually producing a huge survey on the topic. There are other examples of architects going from their own country to work in another, and doing so in a respectful, sympathetic way.

D T   How was the reception of "Towards a Critical Regionalism" at the time it was published?

K F   In the *Collected Essays* of Alan Colquhoun, there are two moments in which he dismisses critical regionalism as "soft leftism."[6] However, landscape was an issue Alan completely neglected. He saw the whole predicament of late modernity as a crisis of architectural syntax independent from topography. I believe landscape is a crucial aspect of regionalist architecture. Behind the theory of critical regionalism—if you can call it a theory—was the practice of figures such as Gino Valle, Oswald Mathias Ungers, and Aris Konstantinidis. In the beginning, my thesis about critical regionalism was well received in Latin America, Spain, and Catalonia, in particular, where Josep Lluis Mateo and Eduard Bru (who jointly edited the Collegi d'Arquitectes de Catalunya magazine *Quaderns*) were sympathetic to critical regionalism. Later, however, after the mid-eighties, they decided it was necessary to move on.

D T   Did you yourself see any limitations in your idea of critical regionalism?

K F   One of the reasons I turned toward tectonics after publishing my essay on critical regionalism is because in one American locality after another, students responded by saying there was nothing regional about the architecture in the region in which they happened to be situated. The fact is, of course, that one may travel enormous distances over the United States and encounter the same pattern of contemporary building, thousands of miles apart. This surely has to do in large measure with widespread air-conditioning and car ownership. *Studies in Tectonic Culture* was the consequence of living and teaching in the United States, where the question of regional architecture was problematic to the point of non-existence.[7] After lecturing extensively on critical regionalism in different places at different times, it was either implied or directly stated that one could no longer conceive of a regional architectural culture in the United States, even though it's an enormous country with different climates.

The concept of tectonics speaks to my interest in the poetics of construction and structure. I went in this direction because I was trying to find a way to exemplify a grounded practice, which, based on materiality, structure, and construction, could also be inflected. The book began with the four Craig Francis Cullivan Lectures I gave at Rice University in 1992, which dealt with Jørn Utzon, Mies van der Rohe, Louis Kahn, and Auguste Perret. I thought that in the work of these four architects you could identify the manifest importance of construction and structure and this common concern for the tectonic became the point of departure for *Studies in Tectonic Culture*, to which I later added other case studies, like Frank Lloyd Wright.

D T   And others like Carlo Scarpa. Scarpa, and Wright to a cer-   64
         tain extent, holds both banners ... there is something of
         critical regionalism in their work and also a clear tectonic
         strain. Can you comment on this? How did the idea of criti-
         cal regionalism filter your view of the architects included
         in *Studies in Tectonic Culture*?

K F   Scarpa is obviously connected to Wright. And, by the way,
Gino Valle had studied with Scarpa in Venice after the Second
World War. So we may find a line that stems from Wright and Scarpa
in the work of Valle.

D T You reencounter many of the heroic architects, meaning that you reengage with their work on a different register in *Studies in Tectonic Culture*, after having gone through the critical regionalist period.

K F Yes, that's right. When I wrote the first edition of *Modern Architecture: A Critical History*, Kahn got mentioned in the chapter on the eclipse of the New Deal, but I don't really think I understood Kahn at that time. Only later, when writing *Studies in Tectonic Culture*, did I become increasingly involved with Kahn. The essay "Louis Kahn and the French Connection," which I published in *Oppositions* in 1980, is the beginning of my real understanding of Kahn.[8] I acquired my understanding of him through Italian critics, who were much more sensitive to the full significance of his work than most Anglo-American critics. In this regard, I am indebted to Alessandra Latour. Wright is also featured in *Modern Architecture: A Critical History*, but my deeper understanding of Wright came through looking at him from the point of view of structure and construction. *Studies in Tectonic Culture* was important for me by virtue of enriching my understanding of these two figures.

D T You also became increasingly interested in Alvar Aalto and, paraphrasing your words, this fascination derives from the notion that he is the twentieth-century architect whose ideas could still be further developed today.

K F Exactly. I am still trying to complete this argument. Take, for instance, Aalto's Enso-Gutzeit building in Helsinki, which I have never written about. [Fig. 17] There is a nineteenth-century Russian Orthodox church alongside it. Aalto chose to build the Enso-Gutzeit offices with a prefabricated reinforced-concrete frame faced in white stone—creating a kind of cellular organization, an orthogonal *brise-soleil* that adds a sort of depth to the façade. In my view, Aalto chose not to use brick because he wanted to distinguish the office building from the brick of the church. It is a very contextual building insofar as it was conceived to be quite distinct from the church. The edges of the building have a fragmented character, and perhaps this fragmentary quality is important. One of the problems with freestanding buildings is that they tend to be autonomous objects that have nothing whatsoever to do with the objects around them. The proposition is that these fragmented edges, in and of themselves, make the building less of a perfect object in relation to the other objects around it. Since it is not self-contained, it is readable as a montage in relation to the other finite object—the "perfect object" of the Russian Orthodox church. Among other things that Aalto still has to offer at this moment in history is the idea that the fragmentary is important for the way it opens up to the rest of the environment, as opposed to some kind of ideal aesthetic and/or technological object.

1   Kenneth Frampton, *Modern Architecture: A Critical History* (London: Thames & Hudson, 1980).
2   Kenneth Frampton, ed., *Modern Architecture and the Critical Present* (London: Architectural Design Profile, 1982).
3   Paul Ricoeur, "Universal Civilization and National Cultures," in *History and Truth* (Evanston, IL: Northwestern University Press, 1965), 271–284.
4   Alexander Tzonis and Liliane Lefaivre, "The Grid and the Pathway. An Introduction to the Work of Dimitris and Suzana Antonakakis," *Architecture in Greece* 15 (1981): 164–178.
5   Kenneth Frampton, "Towards a Critical Regionalism: Six Points for an Architecture of Resistance," in *The Anti-Aesthetic: Essays on Postmodern Culture*, ed. Hal Foster (Port Townsend, WA: Bay Press, 1983), 16–30.
6   Alan Colquhoun, *Collected Essays in Architectural Criticism* (London: Black Dog, 2009), 280–286 and 287–291.

7   Kenneth Frampton, *Studies in Tectonic Culture: The Poetics of Construction in Nineteenth and Twentieth Century Architecture* (Cambridge, MA: MIT Press, 1995).

8   Kenneth Frampton, "Louis Kahn and the French Connection," *Oppositions* 22 (Fall 1980): 21–53.

Fig. 13   Poster for the exhibition *The Presence of the Past* at the 39th Venice Architecture Biennale, Italy,
           1980, with the view along the Strada Novissima in the Corderie Arsenale. Courtesy of Marsilio Editori.

Fig. 14   Hans Hollein's façade for Strada Novissima for the exhibition *The Presence of the Past* at the 39th
          Venice Architecture Biennale, Italy, 1980. Courtesy of the Private Archive Hollein.

69

October 31, 2011

D   T   Daniel Talesnik
K   F   Kenneth Frampton

D T The last time we talked you were on your way to give a lecture in Ireland. What buildings did you end up showing to
illustrate architects working outside their native contexts
in a respectful, sympathetic way?

K F I showed Álvaro Siza's Iberê Camargo museum in Porto
Alegre, and also his housing project in Schilderswijk in the Netherlands—an example of low-rise terrace housing faced in brick with
pierced picture windows—in order to demonstrate how Siza produced a kind of *répétition différente* within the Dutch tradition,
together with the somewhat idiosyncratic use of stone revetment
adjacent to the entrance—which was, in part, a reference back to
his own formal language. Clearly, the scale of the building and the
brick facings are an allusion to the Dutch public-housing tradition, as
we find this in places like Amsterdam South in the interwar period.

Then I spoke about two Finnish examples. The first was the
Kahere Eila Poultry Farming School in Guinea, West Africa, designed
by the Finnish architecture practice Heikkinen-Komonen. [Fig. 18]
This project is part of a fascinating story in itself, related to its
patron, Eila Kivekäs, a wealthy Finnish woman who had studied economics and anthropology before becoming preoccupied with development in West Africa. In Helsinki she met Alpha A. Diallo, a scholar
from Guinea who had translated the Finnish epic poem *Kalevala*
into Fula, one of the indigenous national languages of Guinea.
Diallo's translation was published in Hungary in 1983 and after he
died in Helsinki in 1984 from a hereditary disease, Kivekäs took it
upon herself to transport his body back to Guinea. She built a house
for herself there, the Villa Eila, also designed by Heikkinen-Komonen, 79
who had previously made a name for themselves in the United
States as the architects of the Finnish embassy in Washington,
DC. [Fig. 19] The Villa Eila consists of a mono-pitch corrugated roof
on rafters, and woven walls on one face to protect the house from
the sun. Kivekäs then commissioned Heikkinen-Komonen to design
the Poultry Farming School in Diallo's memory. Diallo believed that
poultry farming was crucial to increase the level of protein con-
sumed in Guinea. The school is articulated-timber construction. It
has mono-pitch roofs and concrete-block walls, which enclose

classrooms and dormitories arranged around a courtyard. The main lecture hall is given a tectonic inflection by virtue of the wire cable that stiffens the main purlins.

The second Finnish example I showed was designed by three women architects: Saija Hollmén, Jenni Reuter, and Helena Sandman. It was the Women's Centre in Rufisque, Senegal, also built out of concrete blocks. [Fig. 20] It is a beautiful courtyard building, painted in red ochre throughout. It is an architecture comprised of only one material and carefully proportioned openings— glass lenses are inserted into the masonry to provide a modicum of cross ventilation.

The last example I showed was the work of the architect Anna Heringer in Raudrapur, a village in northern Bangladesh: the Modern Education and Training Institute (METI) School, made out of mud and bamboo by local labor. [Fig. 21] Heringer is an Austrian architect who was a Loeb Fellow at Harvard. At the time she was working on her first Bangladesh project, she was a student at the Kunstuniversität in Linz. She has built two buildings in Bangladesh using local craftsmen and laborers. For me, this was a way of expanding the idea of critical regionalism beyond its initial formation; above all the possibility of sensitively applying a sensibility cultivated in one place to another.

D T   In your use of the word "sensibility," I also read an environmental consciousness of place. There is a different sense of environmentalism in your descriptions—it appears to go beyond the general premise of environmental protection and also engages issues of identity. Or perhaps you are referring to a "social sustainability," what I would describe as a relationship between the building of architecture and social structures. Considering the current ubiquity of the concepts of environmentalism and sustainability, do you have a different reading of them?

K F   I have some thoughts about this with regards to the concept of the vernacular. Vernacular building is closely linked to agriculture; it is the work of pre-professional architects or builders; it is built by local craftsmen, and even, in some instances, by the community itself. I am stressing this because the vernacular has strong links to sustainability. There are ironies in all this. For example, take the traditional Japanese house of extremely lightweight, uninsulated construction: in the summer and in a humid climate it worked perfectly in terms of ventilation, but in the cold of winter the only heat was provided by a fire pit in the center of the room. This, plus hot sake, was the way a family kept warm in the winter—one simply went to bed covered by duvets. You were either surrounded by blankets with your feet near the pit or you were in bed. Here you have an example of a vernacular, which, from the point of view of heat in winter, was only sustainable in an uncomfortable way. On the other hand, northern European thick-walled houses with small or moderately sized windows are more sustainable by definition if you consider energy use in relation to the climate. The courtyard house of the Middle East tended to function as a climatological flywheel insofar as it was cooler in the summer and warmer in the winter. There are many different examples of simple building forms, which were more or less sustainable. I am thinking of the use of wind towers in India and the Middle East to catch the breeze and take it down into the lower level of the house. In the case of India, one lived at different levels, on the roof in the hot-wet season, and in the cellar to avoid the heat in the hot-dry season. So the movement of the body through the structure was also a means to render the house sustainable.

D T   But also embedded in this idea of social sustainability is an urban project, and perhaps it does not have to do so much with what we have understood as "green architecture" but with this "other" reading of environmentalism and social issues. I think you are also trying to touch upon those things. For instance, in some of the projects you include in the last edition of *Modern Architecture*, you make the point that there is a fundamental cultural shift from the mass housing of 1945–1975 subsidized by the European welfare states, to the period after 1970, when the housing market takes over. Perhaps there will be a return to the 1945–1975 position, where the state will again take charge of the housing problem, and the idea of sustainability and environmentalism will not only be understood in terms of greenness and performativity, two terms that have been cultivated to follow the logic of the market, but also in terms of culture and a way of life.

K F   It is possible to see the present crisis of capitalism as indicative of fundamental contradictions. The current economic crisis combined with climate change points to the long-term negentropic contradictions built into late capitalism. With the collapse of the Soviet Union and with the rise of a technocratic market economy in the Chinese People's Republic, one witnesses a triumphant capitalism. It is as if there is no other system available for the organization of human society and economy, particularly in the light of the tragic failure of the socialist project in the twentieth century. Although it is sufficiently reasonable to have a rather despairing outlook on the future prospects of our species, it seems to me that this issue of sustainability represents a point of departure from which we may build a fragmentary alternative to the present impasse. In the critical regionalist thesis, I tried to argue that this act of resistance was not only cultural but also political: the idea that a small unit would be able to resist the globalized system to some extent.

In India there is a very interesting woman named Vandana Shiva, who, among other things, has spent the last twenty years of her life fighting against the use of genetically altered seeds. She is against Monsanto's monopoly, particularly because it does not permit native farmers to save seeds. The company sells farmers genetically modified seeds that work for one crop and then the farmer has to buy more from the same source, although he could, in principle, replant the genetically modified seeds. In other words, Monsanto maintains a contractual right over its seeds.[1] She has been struggling for a long time for the right of farmers to keep some seeds each year to reseed their land. Her effort, which may seem quixotic, has got to do with resisting the dictates of global corporate capitalism. There is an Austrian economist, jurist, and political scientist named Leopold Kohr, whose 1957 book *The Breakdown* of Nations argues against large states, and perhaps his ideas are also compatible with my concept.[2] All of this is related to Ernst Friedrich Schumacher, whose phrase "small is beautiful" came from Kohr, who had been his teacher. The subtitle of Shumacher's 1973 book *Small is Beautiful* says everything: *Economics as if People Mattered*.[3] This is close to Ezra J. Mishan's 1967 book, *The Cost of Economic Growth*.[4] In the third chapter of his 1994 book *The Seeds of Time*, Frederic Jameson criticizes critical regionalism from a Marxist standpoint.[5] [Fig. 22] While he is fully aware of what I have been trying to posit, he nonetheless maintains local resistance cannot be sustained against the onslaught of global capitalism.

1   In 2018 the American agro-chemical company Monsanto was acquired by the crop-science division of Bayer, the German pharmaceutical and life-sciences company. Monsanto is known as a major producer of pesticides and genetically modified seeds.

2   Leopold Kohr, *The Breakdown of Nations* (London: Routledge & Kegan Paul, 1957).

3   Ernest Friedrich Schumacher, *Small is Beautiful: Economics as if People Mattered* (New York: Harper & Row, 1973).

4   Ezra J. Mishan, *The Cost of Economic Growth* (London: Staples, 1967).

5   Fredric Jameson, *The Seeds of Time* (New York: Columbia University Press, 1994).

Fig. 20

Hollmén Reuter Sandman Architects, Women's Centre in Rufisque, Senegal, 2001. Photograph by Helena Sandman. Courtesy of Hollmén Reuter Sandman Architects.

89

Fig. 22   Cover of the first edition of Frederic Jameson, *The Seeds of Time* (New York: Columbia University Press, 1994).

June 26, 2012

D T   Daniel Talesnik
K F   Kenneth Frampton

D T   Why did you decide to study architecture?

K F   There are artisans on both sides of my family going well back into the nineteenth century, and possibly further back than that. On one side they were employed in industry, as pattern or tool makers, on the other side they were carpenters. My paternal grandfather was a small contractor who erected houses in the interwar period. My father and his brother inherited the family business, which remained active during the Second World War, and largely involved maintaining government buildings.

During the war, we lived on the edge of London at a boundary between suburbia, local horticulture, and small-scale agriculture. I was attracted to agriculture. After my School Certificate, I opted to go into agriculture—much to the dismay of my art teacher. My parents were very permissive, and while I was their only child, they never put any pressure on me. There was no tradition of agriculture in my immediate family so I worked as an apprentice for two years. Before the age of twenty I had already experienced enough intense physical labor to realize that there was no room for anything else when one worked in the field. One came back from work in the evening and ate and went to sleep. The work was totally exhausting. There was no space for any kind of cultural life, and I realized in the end that I could not deal with this. I shifted to architecture because I possessed some artistic talent, although the fact that my father was a builder may have had something to do with it. In any case, I went to the Guildford School of Art for one year and then, in 1950, I was a successful candidate for the Natural Asphalt Council Scholarship to the Architectural Association (AA) in London where I studied for the next five years.

D T   Was there anyone in particular at the Guildford School of Art that was especially formative for you? Why did you move from Guildford to the AA?

K F   A local architect named Brownjohn directed the department of architecture in the art school. The Trades Union Headquarters in London designed by David du R. Aberdeen was under construction at the time and the job captain on that building was someone named Peter Hatton. He came down from London to the Guildford

School once a week and taught studio. It was a small department, no more than ten students at most. I remember being impressed by this young professional figure in his three-piece suit. Hatton was a Bartlett graduate, as was Brownjohn, so at the Guildford School of Art there was no link to the AA.

D   T   How is it then that you applied for a scholarship to the Architectural Association and not to the Bartlett School of Architecture?

K   F   In the fifties, the AA was quite different from the Bartlett. The latter was still influenced by the École des Beaux-Arts. In fact, the leading Bartlett professors, Albert Richardson and Hector Corfiato, were both Beaux-Arts trained. The technical reason, however, is that there were two academic thresholds in the British educational system and I had only passed the first before going into agriculture. I would have needed two more years in school and would have needed to take an exam that was then called the Higher School Certificate. I could not go to the Bartlett, which is part of University College London, because I did not have the required qualification. Since the Architectural Association was not a university, this requirement was disregarded.

London and the AA were very formative for me. There were a number of young architects teaching in the first year who were working at that time on the Festival of Britain—Leonard Manasseh, for example, who was extremely sophisticated, something of an architectural dandy. We were also taught in the second year by the Architects' Co-Partnership. Toward the end of my five years at the AA, Peter Smithson was teaching. There was also the very impressive figure of Arthur Korn who was a German émigré and the author of the 1953 book *History Builds the Town*.[1] He had been a colleague of Ludwig Hilberseimer in Berlin and when I went to the States he wrote me a letter of introduction to Hilberseimer, which I am ashamed to admit I never used.

The people I met during that period at the AA were, and still are, my closest friends—like John Miller, for example, whom I met at the AA and who was Alan Colquhoun's partner for the best part of his career.

D T　Did the Festival of Britain and the fact that all those build-
　　　ings were being built at the time have any impact on you?[2]
　　　Were students going to see the construction site?
K F　I do not recall making site visits to the Festival of Britain, but
the impact of the finished work was in some way decisive. I have
only recently realized the extent to which this exhibition was influenced by the Stockholm Exhibition of 1930. On the one hand, it was
shaped by the populism at Stockholm. On the other hand, as in
Stockholm, the Festival of Britain hosted a number of avant-garde
works, notably the Skylon, designed by Philip Powell and John
Hidalgo Moya, and engineered by Felix Samuely, which was a lightweight "cigar-shaped" metal construction suspended in space by
wire cables. [Fig. 23] The Dome of Discovery by Ralph Tubbs was
of a similar genre, a "flying saucer" kind of building, supported by
inclined lattice columns around the perimeter of the dome. Both of
these works were recognizably avant-garde, and would be so even
now. Then the third building that was important, and still remains
important today, considering the other two were demolished, is the
Royal Festival Hall designed by Peter Moro and Leslie Martin.[3] The
result suggests to me that the design was primarily by Moro, who
had previously worked for Berthold Lubetkin, which accounts for
the Lubetkin-like syntax of the building. I think, even today, that
the handling of the public space below the belly of the auditorium
is exceptional, and it remains as an astonishingly dynamic space
of movement and promenade.
D T　In relation to your period at the AA, how did it happen that
　　　you studied in the Department of Tropical Architecture?
　　　Was it within the five years that you mention?[4]
K F　Yes, it was within those five years, because in the fourth
year we were given the option of being "guinea-pig" students for
the first year of the Department of Tropical Architecture. They gave
us this option instead of the normal fourth-year curriculum and it
was extremely productive to work with Jane Drew and Maxwell Fry.
[Fig. 24] They set very simple studio problems for the trial year; one
was a house in a hot-dry climate—in effect, India—the other was a
house in a hot-wet climate—that is to say, West Africa. These houses

97

had to take into consideration extreme climatic conditions. The one in India was more complex, because of the mixture between the hot-dry season and the monsoon climates, as opposed to say just the hot-wet climate, as in West Africa. In the Indian case, the occupant moves down in the extremely hot season and up again at night, particularly in the humid conditions of the monsoon. And, of course, one had to protect the house from heavy rain, whereas in West Africa one put the emphasis on cross ventilation and lightness. You must remember that in the fifties it was not assumed that these houses would be air-conditioned. The comfort levels had to be achieved by natural means. So maybe these experiences were later an influence on my evocation of critical regionalism.

D T In hindsight, would you see the Department of Tropical Architecture at the AA as an early contribution to what has now become the issue of "sustainability" in architecture? In being critical about how you were deploying these low-tech, passive strategies, was there an awareness of reinvention or reengineering of intermediate technologies?

K F In England in the fifties, the AA's Department of Tropical Architecture was a post-colonial reflex, and one of the overwhelming factors, I think, was the assumption that air-conditioning was not a universal panacea and that it could not be made available worldwide—and that, perhaps, individual air-conditioning was not even desirable. These studio experiences were before Reyner Banham celebrated Willis Carrier as the American inventor of the one-off autonomous air-conditioning unit that, like the automobile, was universally available for everybody. So sustainability was there, but we never used that term. In the *New York Times* there was an article on the escalation of air-conditioning in India at this moment, with all of the negative consequences in terms of electricity consumption and the way in which hot air is exhausted back into the city, creating the infamous "heat-island effect."[5]

98

D T What did you do after the Architectural Association?

K F For a brief period I worked for Chamberlin, Powell and Bon, the architects that had won the Golden Lane competition, and I worked on Golden Lane, but only very briefly, for a summer.[6]

[Figs. 25–26] Then I had to go into the British Army because up to that point I had been deferred, first by working in agriculture and then by being a student. Once I graduated, this deferment was terminated, so I spent the next two years of my life in the Royal Engineers. Apart from the basic training, it was a wasted two years. I was stationed in the West Country in a place called Bovington in Dorset, and was engaged in ridiculous drafting work in an engineering office. I happened to be in the army at the time of the Suez Crisis of 1956–1957, and once I got out, I went to Israel.

D T And you went to Israel because of a work prospect?

K F At the Architectural Association I became friends with a fellow student named Ram Karmi, who was an Israeli, and later I became involved with his wife's younger sister. I went to Israel in pursuit of her. I worked in Tel Aviv with Ram and his father, Dov Karmi, in their practice Karmi-Melzer-Karmi. Later I worked for the Tel Aviv partnership of Itzhak Yashar and Dan Eytan.

D T So it was a very active work period in Tel Aviv?

K F It was very formative for me, since the building technology there was very simple—basically reinforced-concrete construction with rendered-concrete block walls. The climate was very easy to deal with and, since there was no air-conditioning, construction was also easy, technologically speaking. That built a lot of confidence in me. One could enter into the production of buildings without too much anxiety. This was particularly liberating.

D T Did you see the work of Arieh Sharon at the time?

K F Yes, he was a very prominent figure since he had made the master plan for the country in the fifties. However, I was more familiar with his son Eldar who was the same generation as Ram Karmi. I was very impressed by Sharon's prewar housing in Tel Aviv.

D T After Israel you returned to London?

K F Yes, where I first worked for Middlesex County Council and then for Douglas Stephen & Partners.

D T Can you describe the move from Middlesex County Council to Douglas Stephen, where you began to develop a project on your own, parallel to your work as technical editor at *Architectural Design*?

K F   It was a very dynamic period for me. Stephen was an eccentric and generous figure, with a lot of energy and charm. He practiced with his wife, Margaret Stephen. The firm employed young architects and gave them a lot of freedom and took a certain risk in doing so. He looked over everybody's shoulder and criticized everything, of course, but in the end he gave one a lot of responsibility. Not just to myself, but also to others, such as Edward Jones, Elia Zenghelis, David Wild, and Michael Carapetian, who was the house photographer for the anthology that Douglas and I edited titled *British Buildings 1960–1964*.[7] [Figs. 27–28] We were all able to achieve small projects designed entirely by ourselves. When I joined *Architectural Design* in 1962, an apartment building that I had designed was still under construction, so I divided my time between *Architectural Design* in the afternoon and Douglas Stephen & Partners in the mornings—a sort of double life.

D T   Can you tell me more about the building you designed in Craven Hill Gardens in London while you were at Douglas Stephen?

K F   The building is now called Corringham, and is located in Bayswater in central London, very close to Kensington Gardens and Hyde Park. [Fig. 29] Since 1998 it has been listed Grade II.[8] I was able to convince the developer to adopt the slightly crazy system of split-level staircases. This gave us forty-eight units with all the bedrooms facing east and all the living rooms facing west, so you would get sun in the bedrooms in the morning and sun in the living rooms in the afternoon. All the apartments are split-level, either up-going or down-going, with the bathrooms always suspended on half-levels between the bedroom and the living room. [Figs. 30–31] This references the Narkomfin apartment building in Moscow, where half-levels are employed to yield one-and-a-half height living spaces. This whole work is related to my interest in Russian Constructivism and in Le Corbusier's interpretation of the Soviet Dom Kommuna, realized in the Unité d'Habitation in Marseille. This extravagant use of split-levels is a kind of spatial weaving, a way of bonding units together—a metaphor, in fact, for forms of collectivity.

D　T　Going back to *Architectural Design*, how did you meet its editor, Monica Pidgeon?

K　F　Through Theo Crosby.

D　T　How does he enter the story?

K　F　I am not quite sure when he migrated from South Africa to the UK—I think in the fifties. And I am also not quite sure when he started to work with Monica on *Architectural Design*. He was certainly there for a good six years or so before I joined as technical editor. Theo left in 1961 to join Taylor Woodrow and to work on Euston Station. He gave that up at the end of 1964, when he joined Pentagram, which had been called Fletcher/Forbes/Gill but changed its name then to Crosby/Fletcher/Forbes. Only later did it become Pentagram. Robin Middleton, who would succeed me at *Architectural Design* in December 1964, worked for Theo on the Euston project. Robin had studied for a PhD under Nikolaus Pevsner at Cambridge, which led to his thesis on Viollet-le-Duc that, unfortunately, was never published.

D　T　What did you bring out of the *Architectural Design* period?

K　F　My time at *Architectural Design* was short, two and a half years, but during that time I had a lot of contact with Zurich—I knew very well Max Bill and Richard Lohse who were both important graphic designers and painters. I became aware through Joseph Rykwert of the work of Gino Valle in Udine, and afterward I went to Germany with Monica Pidgeon. There I met Oswald Mathias Ungers in Cologne, whom I already knew about through a special issue of *Casabella* edited by Ernesto Rogers that featured his early work.[9] Aris Konstantinidis I knew through Panos Koulermos who introduced us in Athens. (Koulermos would play a crucial role in the early days of my stint in the Stephen office). We did a special issue on Valle and half a special issue on Konstantinidis. The seeds of critical regionalism, if you like, were already implicitly in place at this moment. I thought at the time, and this, of course, was partly fanciful fiction on my behalf, that there was a particular connection between these architects and the cities in which they happened to be situated.

　　It made me aware, first of all, that provinciality can be found everywhere. In both a positive and negative aspect; the negative aspect being when a particular place thinks it is the center of the world. To strive for a cultural autonomy while taking the whole world into consideration, is, in my view, a positive provinciality. I became interested in Europe when I was at *Architectural Design*. I had at the time the idea that in Europe certain city-states were still in place as centers of local identity; for example, in Cologne the city gained an identity due to the work of Ungers, a similar situation obtained in Udine because of Valle, in Zurich because of Ernst Gisel, and in Athens because of Konstantinidis. These were architects who each had an intimate connection with the provincial city in which they worked. When I compared their situation to the British provincial cities, I could not think of a single occasion in which there was an equally strong cultural connection between an architect of talent and a particular city. If you look at *Architectural Design* under my brief editorship, there is an emphasis on that. I tried to push the journal toward a stronger awareness of Europe.

D T Do you think this is a generation in Europe that subverts, as a direct consequence of the Second World War, the prewar tendency of architects that worked all over Europe? I am thinking of Le Corbusier's international career; Mies, with projects in at least three European countries; Erich Mendelsohn, and so on. Whereas Ungers, Valle, and Konstantinidis rooted themselves, in the beginning at least, to single cities, mainly the places or regions they were from.[10]

K F I still think that the best work Ungers achieved in his life was the work he did in Cologne, in brick, before he went to Berlin. [Fig. 32] I am thinking about some of his "infill" apartment buildings, and also about his own house in Belvederestraße, which was slightly influenced by Dutch neoplasticism, but was not avant-garde otherwise. I mean the influence largely showed itself in the pinwheel formation of the plan.

D T There was an editorial shift in *Architectural Design* when you left the journal and came to the United States. When Robin Middleton became technical editor, we started to see Archigram published in the magazine.

K F   Except for publishing Michael Webb's Sin Palace, which I greatly admired, I always kept my distance from Archigram. In fact, Archigram was virtually excluded in the magazine when I was there. When Middleton arrived, he was much more amenable to Archigram and to Cedric Price.

D T   When you lived in London, where did the conversations about architecture take place?

K F   In Soho, in the center of London, there was a public house called the York Minster, which still exists. During the war it had been where the Free French used to gather, so it was popularly known as the "French Pub."[11] [Fig. 33] Every Saturday morning, a certain circle would form there around James Stirling. This group included Douglas Stephen, Robert Maxwell, Alan Colquhoun, Kit Evans, Alan Forest, and myself. The other crucial figure in the circle was Thomas "Sam" Stevens, who, as it happened, would recommend Hannah Arendt to me. He was a polymath who had taught Colin Rowe in Liverpool. He had studied history of art at the Courtauld Institute, where he got his BA, and he then taught history at the Architectural Association. Stevens was like Mark Cousins, someone who could teach without notes. He was an enormous influence on people like Colquhoun, Stirling, Rowe, and myself. Sam was the connection that enabled me to teach undergraduate architectural history and theory at Princeton, without any specific academic qualifications. At Princeton, for me, the Dewey principle of learning through doing meant learning by teaching. I became adept in the material by virtue of teaching it.

D T   Did you know Reyner Banham at that time?

103

K F   A little. But we were in different circles. There was the circle around the Independent Group with Alison and Peter Smithson and Banham. And there was the circle more focused around James Stirling, which included the aforementioned group in Soho, plus John Miller and Edward Jones. So while we were familiar with Banham, we were critical of him. I suppose you could say that we agreed with Colquhoun's critique of Banham that he set forth in his review of *Theory and Design in the First Machine Age*, which appeared in the *British Journal of Aesthetics* when the book came out.[12] We were skeptical of Archigram and of the British High-Tech movement that emerged out of Archigram, two things ideologically linked to Banham.

1   Arthur Korn, *History Builds the Town* (London: Lund Humphries, 1953).

2   The Festival of Britain in 1951 was intended to celebrate the centenary of London's Great Exhibition at the Crystal Palace. However, rather than being international like the 1851 event, this version, as its name suggests, became a celebration of British postwar culture and identity. The main site was the South Bank of the Thames (now housing the National Theatre, the Hayward Gallery, and the Royal Festival Hall) but there were specialized events in other places, such as the *Live Architecture* exhibition at the Lansbury Estate in Poplar, East London. This area was chosen because almost a quarter of its buildings had been destroyed or damaged in the Second World War; after the war, the Lansbury Estate became the focus of an urban regeneration scheme. The Susan Lawrence School was one of the early buildings to be

reconstructed and its design was introduced as a "living example" of postwar planning and architecture.

3   London County Council's chief architect, Robert Matthew, was officially in charge of the Royal Festival Hall; architect Edwin Williams also worked on the project with Martin and Moro.

4   The Department of Tropical Architecture was established at the Architectural Association in 1954 by Jane Drew, Maxwell Fry, and James Cubitt and operated there until 1971 when it was transferred to the University of London. It offered studies and methods on colonial planning and housing in North and West Africa, the West Indies, and India. According to Marion von Osten, "It taught and reflected the 'new' role of the western architect in the global South, building and teaching methods and climate specific materials and construction techniques before the background of the emerging international development aid programs in the era of decolonization." The program is perhaps best known for the leadership of Otto Königsberger, who transformed it into a think-tank for architectural and planning solutions for development aid programs. See Marion von Osten, "A Hot Topic: Tropical Architecture and Its Aftermath," *Fall Semester*, 2014, https://static1.squarespace.com/static/56ec53dc9f7266dd86057f72/t/581f40224402439b560ff56e/1478443043626/BookletMVO-online.pdf. See also Architectural Association, "Department of Tropical Architecture," London (prospectus, 1954).

5   Elisabeth Rosenthal, "My Air-Conditioner Envy," *New York Times*, June 21, 2012.

6   The Golden Lane competition was launched by the City of London in 1951 for the design of new council housing, comprising apartment units in a variety of different sizes. The site was located to the north of Cripplegate in London, which had been destroyed by German bombing during the Second World War. Geoffrey Powell won the competition to build the estate in February 1952 and subsequently formed the Chamberlin, Powell and Bon partnership to develop the project (Powell, along with architects Peter "Joe" Chamberlin and Christoph Bon had a prior agreement that if any of them won the competition, they would share the commission). The competition is also renowned for the entry by Alison and Peter Smithson; while it was unsuccessful, the proposal for "streets-in-the-air"—elevated housing "decks" that could each support ninety families—entered the disciplinary canon. See Peter and Alison Smithson, *The Charged Void: Urbanism* (London: Monacelli, 2005), 26.

7   Douglas Stephen, Kenneth Frampton, and Michael Carapetian, *British Buildings 1960–1964* (London: Adam and Charles Black, 1965), 80–85.

8   Grade II refers to one of four statutory listings established by Historic England, an official government body that protects buildings and structures of specific architectural or historical interest from certain alterations or destruction.

9   See Aldo Rossi, "A Young German Architect: Oswald Mathias Ungers," *Casabella* 244 (1960): 22–36.

10   Gino Valle (1923–2003) was born and raised in Udine, where, in 1951, he started Studio Architetti Valle with his brother Nani, continuing the practice established by their father, Provino, in the twenties. Oswald Mathias Ungers (1926–2007) was born in Kaisersesch in West Germany; he studied in Karlsruhe between 1947 and 1950 when he set up a practice in Cologne and later opened offices in other German cities. Aris Konstantinidis (1913–1993) was born and raised in Athens. He studied architecture in Munich between 1931 and 1936 when he returned to Athens. There he worked in the Town Planning Department and for the Greek Ministry of Public Works while operating a private practice. The Weekend House in Anavyssos (1962–1964) is one of his landmark buildings.

11   The York Minster's name was officially changed to "The French House" in 1984.

12   Review by Alan Colquhoun, *British Journal of Aesthetics* (January 1962), reprinted in Joan Ockman ed., *Architecture Culture, 1943–1968: A Documentary Anthology* (New York: Rizzoli, 1993), 343.

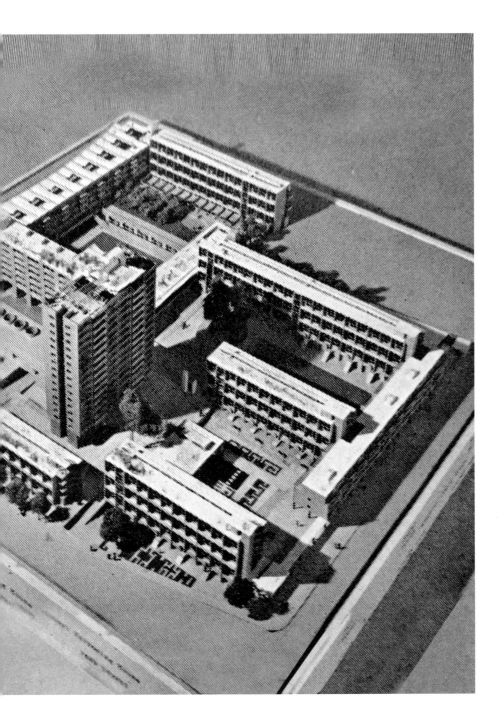

111

Fig. 26   Alison and Peter Smithson, Golden Lane Estate competition, London, 1952. Courtesy of the Frances
          Loeb Library; Harvard University Graduate School of Design.

Fig. 27   Cover of Douglas Stephen, Kenneth Frampton, and Michael Carapetian, *British Buildings 1960–1964*
           (London: Adam and Charles Black, 1965).
Fig. 28   Sir Leslie Martin, Harvey Court, Gonville & Caius College, Cambridge, England, 1960–1962.
           Photograph by Michael Carapetian. As published in Stephen, Frampton, and Carapetian, *British
           Buildings 1960–1964*, 50.

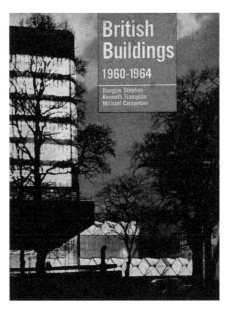

113

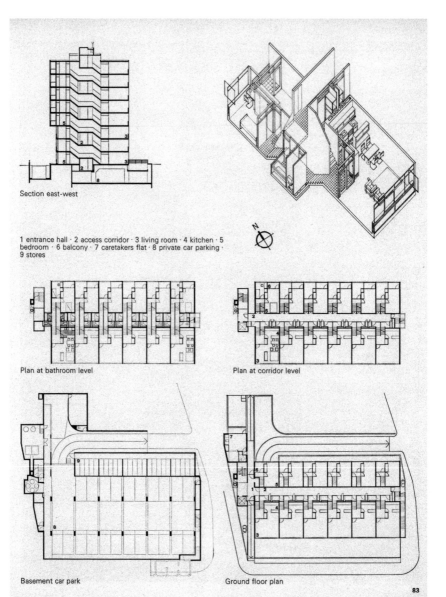

Section east-west

1 entrance hall · 2 access corridor · 3 living room · 4 kitchen · 5 bedroom · 6 balcony · 7 caretakers flat · 8 private car parking · 9 stores

Plan at bathroom level

Plan at corridor level

Basement car park

Ground floor plan

83

116

Fig. 31   Kenneth Frampton (project architect), Douglas Stephen & Partners, Corringham housing complex, 13–15 Craven Hill Gardens, Bayswater, London, 1962–1964. Photograph by Michael Carapetian. As published in Stephen, Frampton, and Carapetian, *British Buildings 1960–1964*, 85.

Fig. 32   Oswald Mathias Ungers, apartment and commercial building, Hansaring 25–27, Cologne, 1959.
            As published in Frampton, *Modern Architecture: A Critical History*, 5th ed., 590.

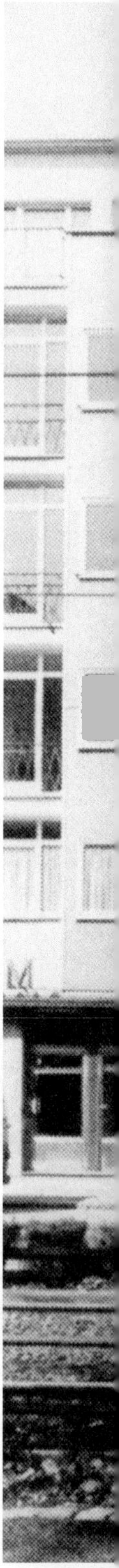

December 17, 2012

D T Daniel Talesnik
K F Kenneth Frampton

D T   When did you start writing about architecture?

K F   My first critical essays were in *Architectural Design*; there was one on James Stirling's Engineering Building at Leicester University, one on the Smithsons' Economist Building in St. James, and one on Hans Scharoun's Berliner Philharmonie.[1] These three essays were my first serious writings on architecture. There were other essays from that period, including a short piece titled "Forty Years of Breuer" that I also wrote for the magazine, but these three are the most important for me from that period.[2] Around that time, I also wrote my first essay on the Maison de Verre, which appeared in the Architectural Association journal, *Arena*.[3]

D T   These early writings coincided, to some degree, with your work on the book *British Buildings 1960–1964*, which was published in 1965, right? Can you speak more about the motivation behind this book?

K F   The book was the result of a collaboration between Douglas Stephen, Michael Carapetian—who did the photographs—and myself. [Figs. 27–28, 30–31 on pages 113, 116–117] Michael is a very exceptional architectural photographer who has never worked professionally as such. He is an architect, and we worked together at Douglas's office in London. The book arose out of the office. It is an anthology of significant British buildings from the early sixties. It features work that might be considered brutalist, given the loose usage of the term. All the projects in the book were realized, and the book included plans, drawings, and descriptions of each that I wrote. Otherwise, it is simply a photographic anthology with an introduction by Hugh Casson and a foreword by Douglas. It still remains, I think, an interesting selection. Douglas dedicated the book to Colin Rowe, whom he had first encountered at the Liverpool School of Architecture where they both studied. Banham's review of this book starts off in a very ironic fashion, something along the lines of: "the average reader probably has no idea who Colin Rowe is."[4] He then proceeds to explain that Rowe is a kind of guru and that the selection of buildings represents the taste of a certain circle. However, in this case, it is fairly eclectic, since the Smithsons are represented by the Economist Building and by an interior that

125

they made for Iraqi Airways within Iraqi House, in London. James Stirling is there with his Leicester University Engineering Building, Alan Colquhoun and John Miller also have a building in the anthology, and there is my own Corringham housing complex that I worked on while in the office of Douglas Stephen & Partners. [Figs. 34–36] Patrick Hodgkinson is featured, also someone of my generation. In fact, both Miller and Hodgkinson were in my year at the Architectural Association. The architects of record for Hodgkinson's building in the book are, in fact, Sir Leslie Martin and Colin St. John Wilson, whom he worked for at the time. However, it is unquestionably Hodgkinson who put that building together, as one may judge by another of his buildings in the book for Lord Adrian in Cambridge, which is credited to him alone. While there are some buildings in the book that one would not associate with brutalism, it does represent a certain moment and a certain time.

D T   Although you wrote many articles after *British Buildings* came out, strictly speaking, your next book is *Modern Architecture: A Critical History*, published in 1980. Before we talk about that book, do you want to say something about pieces written between 1965 and 1980?

K F   There was an essay that you could say was rather unusual for its time, published in 1968 in *Architectural Design*, called "The Humanist versus the Utilitarian Ideal," that deals with Hannes Meyer and Le Corbusier's entry for the League of Nations.[5] [Figs. 37–38] This piece informed much of the approach taken in *Modern Architecture*—especially in the chapters on the "New Objectivity" and "Le Corbusier." By the time *Modern Architecture* was published, at least one of the two special issues of *Oppositions* I edited that were dedicated to Le Corbusier had already been published.[6] The material of these issues was not only by myself but also by contributors like Robert Slutzky, Mary McLeod, Stanislaus von Moos, Steven Hurtt, and Alexander C. Gorlin. All of this had an influence on the chapters devoted to Le Corbusier in my history. However, much of the material of *Modern Architecture* was specially written for the book and had not been previously worked out in the form of an essay.

D T   How did the idea of writing *Modern Architecture: A Critical History* come about?

K F   It was a direct commission from Robin Middleton, then the acquisitions editor for Thames & Hudson. I think I signed the contract in 1970, so it took me ten years to produce the book. By 1970 I was full-time at Princeton University. I did not come to Columbia University until 1972. I was at Columbia from 1972 to 1974, and then I went back to England from 1974 until 1977, so the book was published a few years after I came back to Columbia. What has always surprised me, in retrospect, is that the first edition of the book appeared the same year as Paolo Portoghesi's postmodern overview at the Venice Biennale: "The End of Prohibitionism."[7] It is still surprising to me that they would coincide. It was also the year of the first Aga Khan award ceremony.[8]

D T   Let's talk in detail about *Modern Architecture: A Critical History*. Who edited the book?

K F   It was edited by Emily Lane, who was a full-time editor for Thames & Hudson. She was an incredibly perceptive editor. There was also a considerable amount of editing by Robin Middleton, but in the end the full responsibility was taken by Lane, who is still alive and active. She is an American who has lived in England almost her entire life. Both Emily and Robin had been pupils of Nikolaus Pevsner.

I should say that the first three chapters were conceived by me, with the first dealing with the Enlightenment and classicism, the second with urbanism, and the third with engineering. These chapters were overseen by experts. The one on "Cultural transformations: Neo-Classical architecture 1750–1900" was overseen by Anthony Vidler and Robin Middleton; the one on "Territorial transformations: urban developments 1800–1909" was overseen by Anthony Sutcliffe; and the one on "Technical transformations: structural engineering 1775–1939" was edited by Pedro Guedes.[9] The contributions made by Vidler, Middleton, Sutcliffe, and Guedes guaranteed, as it were, the probity of these chapters.

D T   The research process must have been complicated, considering the vast scope of the material. Reyner Banham's *Theory and Design in the First Machine Age* (1960) derives from his dissertation under Nikolaus Pevsner, which took him a number of years to turn into a book.[10] [Fig. 39] But your book was like a dissertation without a supervisor. Today it would be unthinkable to do a comprehensive modern history of architecture as a dissertation topic but in the mores of that period, one could attribute your book to a certain relaxed climate.

K F I suppose so. The important figure in the generation of this book was Middleton, who brought it into existence, and it was his confidence in me that led to its being carried through. Moreover, his editing—in addition to Emily's—allowed me to complete the book. I internalized Robin's voice. The World of Art series of Thames & Hudson had a set dimension and size, and to write about the history of modernity in such a limited format was a real challenge—I was always trying to deal with too much material. This is part of the reason it took ten years to produce. Robin was constantly saying to me: "you don't need this sentence, you have said it already" or "you don't need this adjective, it adds nothing to the concept." He was always invariably right, and so was Emily. The one thing that defines the character of the writing is its density, which makes it a somewhat daunting book for students. Each sentence adds to the one before, and there is no rhetorical repetition. Everything progresses the argument forward—without repetition. Left to my own devices, I would probably not have written it like that. But Robin's voice would never leave my head. Thanks to him, I developed a capacity to edit my own material. I can see when something is not clearly and economically formulated, when the words are not precise, or when things should be turned around for clarity. As a result, the only way I can write is through editing and reediting; thus, a first draft, a second, a third, and even a fourth, for every article.

D T In other words, in the process of writing and reacting to the editing of *Modern Architecture: A Critical History*, you acquired a method that you have applied since then?

K F Right. This is central, because in my experience thinking and writing are inseparable. The act of writing is in itself an attempt to clarify thought. In other words, the language also thinks the writer. It is clear that the language is ever present as are the limits of the language—both the limits of the writer and the writing. Colin Rowe, for instance, uses language in a way that I am incapable of doing. Despite the fact that his sentences are long, he is exceptionally elegant and witty. One gets this even more strongly when reading literature; certain writers are able to embody a particular image, a narrative, or a characterization that is emerging out of the writing itself, and virtually can't be imitated.

D T I am interested in the subsequent editions of *Modern Architecture: A Critical History* and how it was updated. Was it planned from the beginning that the book might have editions?

K F No, it was not. The initiative to produce new editions came from Thames & Hudson—that is to say, from Thomas Neurath. I suppose the book was the most successful within the World of Art series. It had a reception and a circulation far greater than any other publication in that series. Thames & Hudson was very interested in maintaining its currency. Neurath told me: "we need a new edition to keep the book alive." I am now working on a fifth edition, and there will be a big change if I manage to survive long enough to complete it. They are going to increase the size of the book and expand the number of pages. It gives me the chance to rework certain chapters and to correct typos and other mistakes, which are not so major, but still irritating. In all the previous editions they would not revise the chapters, but just add new chapters. Now they are open to a full revision, within limits. So, for instance, the Czech modern movement, which is more or less absent from the book, will have a chapter of its own. Then, China and India will appear for the first time, and the Nordic chapter on Alvar Aalto and National Rationalism may be broken into two chapters, and so on. In the French version of the fourth edition, I wrote a chapter dealing with the French modern movement between the wars, and thus the Maison de Verre, previously excluded, will finally appear in this chapter. As of now, this is only in the French edition, which is an anomaly.

129

D T It is unavoidable to group *Modern Architecture: A Critical History* with Banham's *Theory and Design in the First Machine*

Age, and William Curtis's *Modern Architecture Since 1900* (1982).[11] They represent three different takes on a similar set of material. How would you position *Modern Architecture* in relation to Banham and Curtis's books—what gap did your book fill?

K F First of all, Banham's thesis has a particular argument to make, and because of that there are certain aspects of the modern movement that are simply left out: Aalto, the Czechs, and, with the exception of El Lissitzky, the Russians don't appear either—which is rather surprising. At the same time, Banham was a big inspiration behind my book; the method of using the protagonist of the moment and allowing him or her to "speak" within the body of the text is one I took directly from him. The big difference is ideological. I think Banham was an incredibly perceptive critic and a brilliant writer. Nevertheless, his populism is present throughout, above all in the way that the book ends with Buckminster Fuller.

D T Banham's search for an origin, for certain protomodern de-velopments—which is marked by adding "other" figures to his early genealogy of the modern movement—brackets his history of modern architecture. He makes present his constant dissatisfaction with architecture's failure to inte-grate technology, or the way it allows it to take over. In your case, you do not appear to have that latent dissatisfaction; rather, you allow yourself to be surprised by what you con-sider to represent a prime development in each historical moment, and highlight how it changed the status of the dis-cipline. Commenting on Le Corbusier—or whomever the chapter is about—you tend to commend what you detect to be the main contribution of each architect. Moreover, you try to understand how this changed the situation around it. In other words, you are concerned with shifts. Perhaps we could use the word "celebratory," even if it's not the most accurate description.

K F To start with, neither Banham nor Curtis were educated as architects, and this makes a difference. I think the fact that I was trained as an architect decisively shaped my approach. I don't know whether to call this "sensibility" or "empathy." With regard to recognizing the intention of an architect or a movement, I think adequate credit has to be given, even if in the end it fails to come through. Even if I acknowledge the movement that can't continue or the cultural wave that has passed, I am nevertheless witness to its intention, and this has to do with my formation as an architect.

D T Immediately after *Modern Architecture: A Critical History* was released, you published two volumes in Japan: *Modern Architecture Vol. 1 1851–1919* and *Modern Architecture Vol. 2 1919–1945*.[12]

K F Yes, and there is no feedback between them. This comes about through Yukio Futagawa, whom I had met in London in 1964 along with Arata Isozaki, when they were touring the world together. I think Isozaki still worked for Urtec under Kenzo Tange at the time, and Futagawa was a photographer who was just beginning to publish. I was very delinquent in producing this material for Futagawa. By the time I finished *Modern Architecture: A Critical History*, I had already been commissioned by Futagawa to do these two volumes. He became incredibly irritated and impatient with me because I was not producing the material fast enough. The volumes in the end have a different character, because they take more of a monographic approach based on single canonical buildings, and these buildings are looked at on their own terms. Some of those buildings do not even appear in *Modern Architecture: A Critical History*. The buildings were selected by Futagawa, in part because he had already photographed them.

D T Considering this was a commission from a Tokyo-based Japanese photographer, it brings to the fore something that I will describe as the "Japanese connection" present in your work as an architectural writer. Not only because of these two books, but later you wrote about Tadao Ando, Arata Isozaki, Kengo Kuma, and so on.

K F Yes, this has been an ongoing interest.

D T One could say that this "Japanese connection" has run parallel to a "Scandinavian connection," which not only accounts for your interest in Aalto, but also in Utzon, Jacobsen, and Lewerentz, among others. But the "Japanese connection" is particular in that you were tasked by the Japanese to write about Japanese architects practicing at the time you wrote about them, and this has its own dynamic.

K F   That is the case and, in this regard, as far as Japan is considered, Isozaki played a crucial role. There was an exhibition in 1978 at the Institute for Architecture and Urban Studies (IAUS) in New York titled "A New Wave of Japanese Architecture," organized by Isozaki.[13] It then traveled to different parts of the country. I should say that Andrew MacNair was the point man for the exhibition and for the "new wave" exhibitions in general. In 1980, the IAUS also exhibited "A New Wave of Austrian Architecture," but the one on Japan was perhaps the more renowned. Anyway, the architects in the show were chosen by Isozaki. It included Tadao Ando, Toyo Ito, Takefumi Aida, Hiromi Fujii, Hiroshi Hara, Osamu Ishiyama, Fumihiko Maki, Monta Mozuna, and Minoru Takeyama. Some of them did not rise to the stardom of Ando and Ito. After this exhibition, Isozaki invited me to Japan, and my wife Silvia and I went together for two weeks as guests of a Japanese foundation. This connection led to the 1989 monograph on the architecture of Isozaki, and eventually to my writings on Ando as well—which were actually published slightly earlier in 1987. Both the Isozaki and Ando publications were commissioned by Futagawa. So, yes, you are right about my "Japanese connection."

In writing *The Architecture of Arata Isozaki*, I was yet again delinquent, so I went to Japan and spent a week holed up in the Yamanoue Hotel in Tokyo.[14] This was Isozaki and Futugawa's idea. I would do the same thing later in Sydney, Australia, when I was writing on Glenn Murcutt. I found it to be an incredible method. I confined myself to this beautiful little hotel in Tokyo, with all the documentation on Isozaki that I could possibly need. The idea was: "you don't come out until you finish the text." It was a great experience.

D T   But would Isozaki come and dine with you? Did you leave the hotel at all?

K F   Basically, I was on my own. They showed up, of course, in the dining room—now and then—but it was really like being in a monastery. There is a sad story attached to this, which has to do with my unreliable character. Namely, my attitude toward Isozaki's Tsukuba Town Hall, which involved a postmodern play on Michelangelo. I was critical of this work, and while Isozaki let it stand and the book was published, it was the end of our friendship. Henceforth, he kept his distance. I remain convinced that his work lost coherence at this point. What he was able to do at Urtec when he worked with Tange, and thereafter in the early years of his own practice, was remarkable.

D T How about the friendship with Isozaki's former protégés?

K F It continued, particularly with Ando, whose work I still greatly admire.

D T Is there anything else you would like to say about *Modern Architecture and the Critical Present*?

K F I might add that Andreas Papadakis, who was the owner of *Architectural Design* in 1980, had a fit of publishing envy and persuaded Thames & Hudson to allow him to publish extracts from the book in *Architectural Design* along with essays by me.[15] It included my essays "The Status of Man and the Status of his Objects," and "The Isms of Architecture," wherein I attempted to classify the pluralism of the late-modern present in terms of "isms" for the first time; hence my personal coinage of "productivism," "rationalism," "structuralism," "populism," and finally "regionalism," as discernable subsets of contemporary practice. I also asked certain critics to review the book.

D T Later, in 1985, your longstanding interest in Pierre Chareau's Maison de Verre in Paris also became a book project.[16] You had already written essays on the house in AA's *Arena* and also in *Perspecta,* where you first published redrawn plans, sections, details, and so on.[17] [Figs. 40–41]

K F Well, before all this, the three main floor plans of the Maison de Verre had been published in the British magazine *Architect and Building News*. It had been drawn and measured by the British architect Margaret Talent, who, if I recall correctly, was working for Candilis, Josic, Woods in Paris at the time. They were hand-drafted following on-site measurements, a first draft in pencil, and then redrawn in ink by hand. This is a technique that Asplund used. When the house was completed around 1931–1932, it was first published in *L'Architecture d'Aujourd'hui*, but only a few sketches and a number of photographs were printed. The plans were never published and this says something about how the building was made. It was a kind of montage building constructed directly from drawings made on site, and it relied on the iron fabricator Louis Dalbet to put the pieces in place.

Then in the fifties, the British came to know the Maison de Verre; James Stirling and Colin St. John Wilson were probably the first Brits to see the house. Later, Richard Rogers would visit it. Meanwhile, the French remained totally uninterested. The first work I did on the house was in 1965, and around that time I met the original owners, Doctor and Madame Dalsace, née Annie Bernheim. Later, in 1966, I received the Hodder Fellowship at Princeton without applying for it; it was arranged by Peter Eisenman. Initially, I had no idea what to do with the grant, but halfway through the semester I thought I might use it to survey the Maison de Verre. I went to Paris with Michael Carapetian and an English colleague, Robert Vickery, to photograph and measure the Maison de Verre on the spot.

There is a Dutch architect named Jan Molema who is pre-occupied with the idea that the Maison de Verre was actually designed by Bernard Bijvoet. Bijvoet's contribution is undeniable, although there are certain aesthetic elements such as the use of iron rods that come from Pierre Chareau. When you look at the overall detailing of the Maison de Verre, it is obvious that Bijvoet played a major role in the resolution of innumerable joints, pivots, and hinges. Molema is currently making an effort to establish this fact. Bearing in mind the work that Johannes Duiker and Bijvoet did together in the Netherlands, and the major work that Bijvoet achieved alone after Duiker's death—specifically the Grand Hotel and Theatre Gooiland in Hilversum (1936)—there is every indication of the influence that Bijvoet had on the Maison de Verre and of the influence that the "luxus" of the Maison de Verre had on him. However, when we all went to Haarlem in the Netherlands to inter-view Bijvoet—the "we" being Madame Vellay Dalsace, Marc Vellay, and myself—Bijvoet insisted that he was just an assistant and that all the big decisions were made by Chareau and Annie Dalsace without his involvement. He would not take credit for anything. We joked afterward that it was like interviewing the general secretary of the Communist party or Harry Lime in *The Third Man*.

D T When was this?

K F In the eighties, because we were ostensibly doing research for a book on Chareau that was to be a collaboration between myself and Mark Vellay.

D T Did you ever visit the house and studio Chareau did for Robert Motherwell in East Hampton (1946) before it was demolished in 1985?

K F No, and that was just laziness. And there were other houses, like his own small house on the Motherwell site, and a strange small house for some lady also in East Hampton and also demolished, I think.

D T I want to move rather quickly through some of your later writing in order to get closer to the present. In 1995, thirty years after you landed here in the United States, you wrote your first book about American architecture: *American Masterworks: The Twentieth-Century House*.[18] How did this book come about?

K F This was a commission from Rizzoli, and I was at liberty to select the buildings. In so doing I committed the sin of excluding the house that Robert Venturi designed for his mother. Robert Stern confronted me and said that I could not possibly do that—that it was outrageous. But Rizzoli refused to be party to any pressure on me, so this house does not appear in the anthology. It was, no doubt, highly regarded by others at the time, but not by me. In general, I was not that convinced of Venturi's position.

D T What about Venturi's scholarship, his publications?

K F There is no question that he is very cultivated, intelligent, informed, etc., but for me, as an architect, he is altogether too mannered, bordering on the cynical. He took a totally opposite stance to that of Louis Kahn. I had more contact with Venturi than with Kahn; however, it took me a long time to come to terms with Kahn. That

135

is why in *Modern Architecture: A Critical History* he only appears in the chapter about "The Eclipse of the New Deal: Buckminster Fuller, Philip Johnson and Louis Kahn 1934–1964." Fuller, Johnson, and Kahn are treated together, along with the Tennessee Valley Authority's spectacular Norris Dam, completed in 1936. The fact is, that when I wrote this chapter I saw Johnson and Kahn as being equally historicist.

D T   I wanted to ask you now about your 2002 book *Labour, Work and Architecture*.[19] What is its connection to the *Human Condition* by Hannah Arendt?

K F   The title is a play on Sigfried Giedion's *Space, Time and Architecture* (1941) and Arendt's remarkable distinction between labor and work, one she claims is present in all languages. I think her discourse remains extraordinarily enlightening for architects. [Fig. 42]

D T   What is the story behind your 2015 *L'altro Movimento Moderno*, which for the moment is only available in Italian?[20]

K F   It is based on a series of lectures I gave in Mendrisio in Switzerland, and the premise is that the received idea of the modern movement is more diverse than the reductive concept of the "white" International Style, as promulgated by Henry Russell Hitchcock and Philip Johnson in 1932. These lectures argue that within the modern tradition there is an unbelievable richness that still requires research and in-depth study. The pedagogical aim was raising the consciousness of students about the legacy of the modern movement as something that is still potentially available for further development.

1   Kenneth Frampton, "Leicester University Engineering Laboratory," *Architectural Design* 34, no. 2 (February 1964): 61; Kenneth Frampton, "The Economist and the Haupstadt," *Architectural Design* 35, no. 2 (February 1965): 61–62; Kenneth Frampton, "Genesis of the Philarmonie," *Architectural Design* 35, no. 3 (March 1965): 111–112.

2   Kenneth Frampton "40 Years of Breuer 1924–64," *Architectural Design* 34, no. 9 (September 1964): 468–470.

3   Kenneth Frampton, "Maison de Verre," *Arena* 81, no. 901 (April 1966): 257–262.

4   Reyner Banham, "In-Architecture Illustrated," *New Society* 7, no. 181 (March 17, 1966): 24–25.

5   Kenneth Frampton, "The Humanist versus Utilitarian Ideal," *Architectural Design* 38 (1968): 134–136.

6   Kenneth Frampton, ed., "Le Corbusier 1933–1960," *Oppositions* 19/20 (Winter/Spring 1980).

7   Paolo Portoghesi, "The End of Prohibitionism," in *The Presence of the Past: First International Architecture Exhibition of the Venice Biennale*, eds. Paolo Portoghesi, Vincent Scully, Charles Jencks, and Christian Norberg-Schulz (Milan: Electa/La Biennale, 1980).

8   The Aga Khan Award for Architecture was established in 1977 to celebrate architectural excellence and reward architectural and design ideas that successfully address the needs and aspirations of Muslim societies. The awards are given every three years, and the first were awarded in 1980 in a ceremony at the Shalimar Gardens in Lahore, Pakistan. The first Chairman's Award (a lifetime-achievement award) was given to Egyptian architect Hassan Fathy and fifteen individual projects were also given prizes. Since its inception, the Aga Khan Award has reflected a concern for regional issues and this perhaps accounts for Frampton's noting it as a relevant event in 1980; his theory of critical regionalism, as noted in an earlier interview, was developed as a counterpoint to the 1980 Venice Architecture Biennale. See Robert Powell, ed., *Regionalism in Architecture*, Proceedings of the Regional Seminar, in *Exploring Architecture in Islamic Cultures 2* (Singapore: Concept Media Pte. Ltd., 1985).

9   Pedro Guedes is the son of the architect Amâncio d'Alpoim Miranda "Pancho" Guedes (1925–2015).

10   Reyner Banham, *Theory and Design in the First Machine Age* (New York: Praeger, 1960).

11   William Curtis, *Modern Architecture since 1900* (Oxford: Phaidon, 1982).

12   Kenneth Frampton and Yukio Futagawa, *Modern Architecture 1851–1919* (Tokyo: A.D.A Edita, 1981); and Kenneth Frampton and Yukio Futagawa, *Modern Architecture 1919–1945* (New York: Rizzoli, 1983).

13   Kenneth Frampton, ed., *A New Wave of Japanese Architecture, September 25, 1978 to November 14, 1978* (New York: Institute for Architecture and Urban Studies, 1978).

14   Yukio Futagawa and Kenneth Frampton, *Arata Isozaki. Vol. 1, 1959–1978* (Tokyo: A.D.A. Edita, 1991).

15   Kenneth Frampton, ed., "AD Profile 42: Modern Architecture and the Critical Present," *Architectural Design* 52 no.7 (December 1982).

16   Marc Vellay and Kenneth Frampton, *Pierre Chareau. Architect and Craftsman 1883–1950* (New York: Rizzoli, 1985).

17   Kenneth Frampton, "Maison de Verre," *Perspecta* 12 (1969): 77–79, 111–128.

18   Kenneth Frampton, *American Masterworks: The Twentieth-Century House* (New York: Rizzoli, 1995).

19   Kenneth Frampton, *Labour, Work and Architecture: Collected Essays on Architecture and Design* (London: Phaidon, 2002).

20   Kenneth Frampton, *L'altro Movimento Moderno* (Mendrisio: Mendrisio Academy Press, 2015). These lectures, written in English, have now finally been published in the original language as *The Other Modern Movement* (New Haven: Yale University Press, 2020).

Fig. 36   James Stirling, Leicester University Engineering Building, Leicester, England, 1959–1963. As published
in Stephen, Frampton, and Carapetian, *British Buildings 1960–1964*, 73.

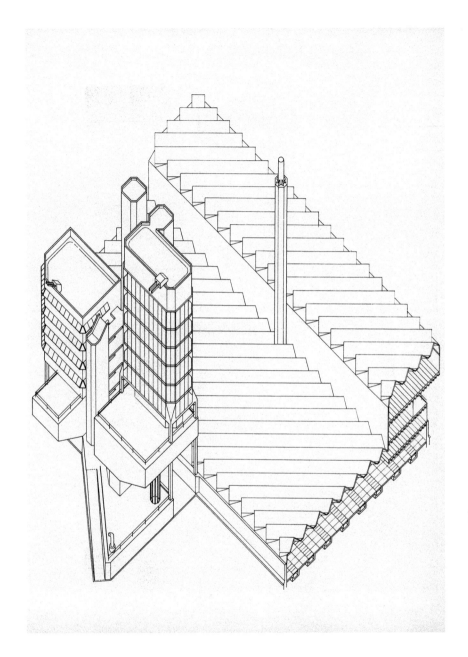

141

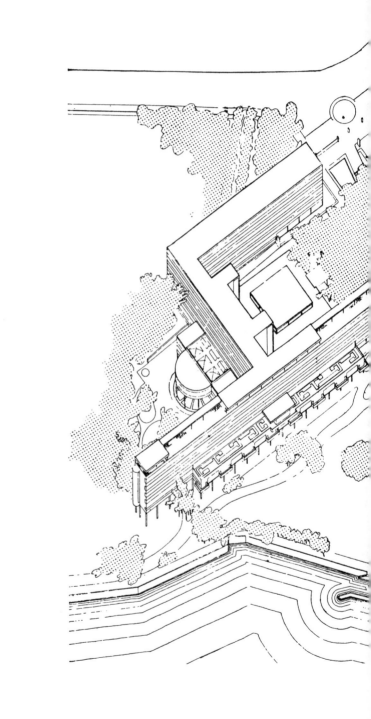

Fig. 37   Le Corbusier, Palace of the League of Nations Competition, Geneva, Switzerland, 1927. As published
in Le Corbusier, *Le Corbusier et Pierre Jeanneret: Ouvre Complète de 1910–1929* (Zurich: Editions
Girsberger, 1943), 163.

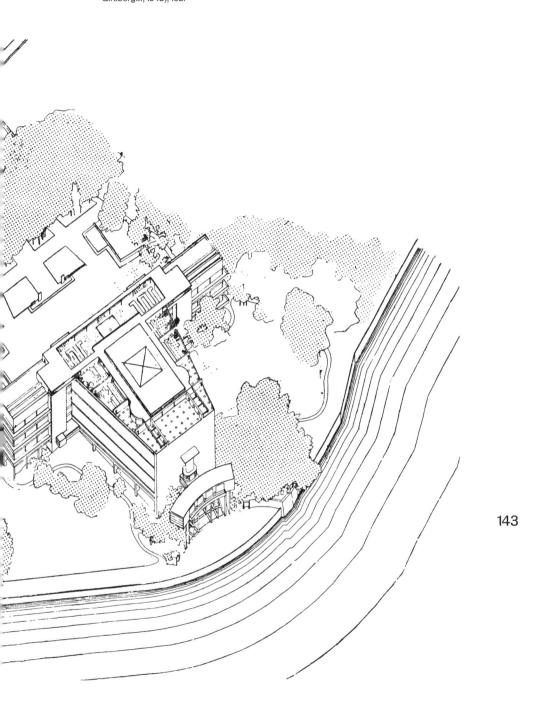

Fig. 38   Hannes Meyer and Hans Wittwer, Palace of the League of Nations Competition, Geneva,
           Switzerland, 1927. As published in Claude Schnaidt, *Hannes Meyer: Buildings, Projects and Writings*
           (Teufen, CH: Arthur Niggli, 1965), 23.

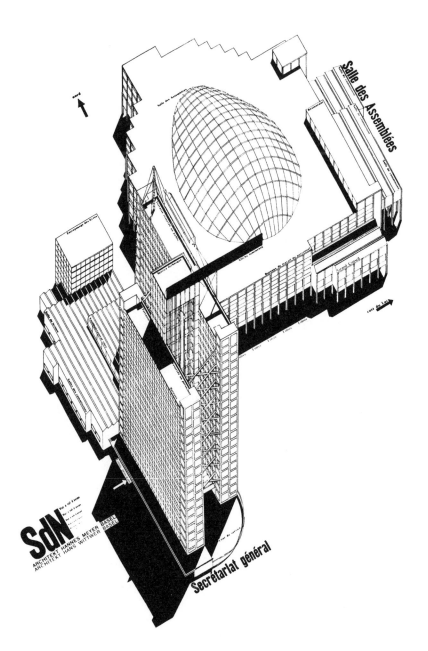

144

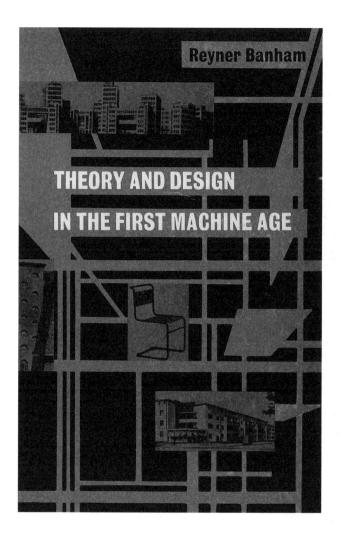

Fig. 41   Pierre Chareau and Bernard Bijvoet, Maison de Verre, 31 Rue Saint-Guillaume, Paris, France, 1928–
1932. Bathroom axonometric by Kenneth Frampton. As published in Kenneth Frampton, "Maison de
Verre," *Perspecta* 12 (1969): 123.

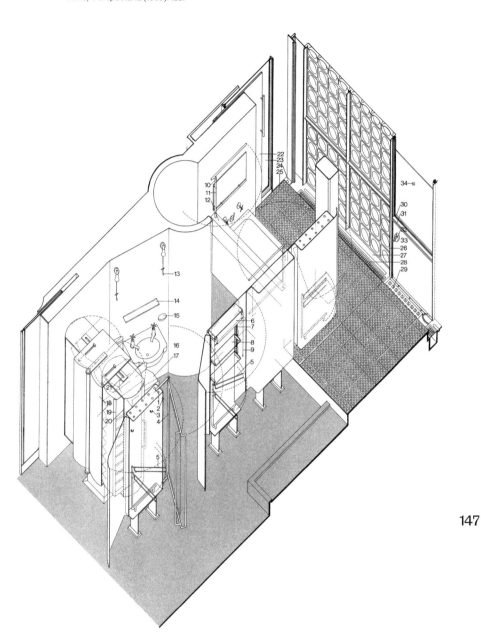

149

January 21, 2013

D T Daniel Talesnik
K F Kenneth Frampton

D T   During the sixties in the British architecture scene, there
        appears to be a division between practicing architects on
        the one hand and historians/critics on the other. Interest-
        ingly, many British architecture historians/critics from your
        generation came to the United States while the practicing
        architects stayed in Britain. This group of architecture
        critics—you among them—brought to the American acade-
        my a different sense of critical thinking, perhaps one that is
        best defined by a greater involvement in building analyses.
        I am thinking of Alan Colquhoun, Robert Maxwell, Anthony
        Vidler, Colin Rowe, and yourself. After this move, you began
        to comment on the British scene, but now from this side
        of the Atlantic. It appears that seeing things from afar gave
        you a certain critical distance.

K F   Coming to the States in the mid-sixties had a paradoxical
effect on me because it politicized me. When I started to study
at the Architectural Association in 1950, I was only twenty years old.
Fifteen years would pass before I first went to the States in 1965.
My early adulthood was in London and I was clearly politically naïve.
I don't think I understood what was at stake or what the issues
were. The English architect Michael Glickman—who belongs to the
same generation as Edward Jones—once said to me: "you have
to understand, in England the claws are hidden but in the States
they are visible." This is an incredible metaphor for the nature and
upfront character of power in the States, which is undeniable.
On the other hand, it is no accident that Cedric Price's client for the
Fun Palace was Joan Littlewood, who ran a left-wing theater in
Stratford in London's East End. She represented the British hard
left—even to the left of Price—on the borders of Communism. With
my *habitués* in England, people like Maxwell and Stirling, or, for
that matter, the Smithsons, and most of the Independent Group, we
were largely apolitical—one could say liberal. There were exceptions
to this, of course—Richard Hamilton being the most telling example
in this regard.

D T   How did you find life in Princeton, New Jersey, during your
        first stint in the United States?

153

K F   Princeton was incredibly stimulating. I had never experienced a "university," strictly speaking, and at Princeton I had a lot
of contact with the Russian department because of my interest
in Russian Constructivism. It was a naïve situation, totally unthinkable by today's standards. Because of Dean Robert Geddes's
Anglophilia, I would, over a short space of time, be appointed to a
full professorship. This appointment was based on nothing other
than my writing and my editing of *Architectural Design*. When I look
back, it is just unreal. Nevertheless, I played a major role in the
school and I had carte blanche in terms of teaching. The fact that
I had not been trained as a historian or theorist says something
about the London architectural scene in the fifties and sixties,
which was totally immersed in the ideology of the modern movement. This is reflected in the fact that when I came to Princeton,
I gave four lectures gratis and ad hoc, on the themes of Futurism,
Purism, Russian Constructivism, and International Constructivism (this last referring to Duiker and Bijvoet and L.C. van der
Vlugt in the Netherlands, and Hannes Meyer and the ABC group
in Switzerland).

D T   Let me ask you something else about that first period at
Princeton—how was the interaction with your colleagues?
Who else was teaching there?

K F   Anthony Vidler arrived soon after me, followed by another
Englishman named Anthony Eardley. Of the two, Tony Vidler was
the more stimulating colleague. When I first arrived, Peter Eisenman
and Michael Graves were already teaching there, although Eisenman
would soon leave after the arrival of Robert Geddes as the new
dean. All the Englishmen that came to Princeton at that time arrived
there on Eisenman's recommendation. The Institute for Architecture and Urban Studies (IAUS) in New York came into being after
Eisenman had left Princeton in 1968. [Fig. 43] I had initially met Peter
in England where he had studied with Colin Rowe at Cambridge.
Tony Vidler was also a student in Cambridge under Rowe when Peter
was an assistant teacher.

D T   And what was the case with Michael Graves? He had earlier
been at the American Academy in Rome.

K F   He had also previously studied at the Graduate School of Design (GSD) at Harvard University. He already had very strong painterly interests. He was always painting, and he would establish his architectural practice at Princeton and remain there until his death in 2015.

D T   What about Jean Labatut?

K F   He was certainly around when I was first there, but he was not a big influence anymore. Other members of the faculty at that time were Heath Licklider, Henry Jandl, and William Shellman. Robert Gutman was also there, serving simultaneously as professor at Rutgers and spending a lot of time at Princeton. He was an adjunct professor and a very interesting figure.

D T   So after coming to the United States and teaching at Princeton for a period, you then returned to England and taught at the Royal College of Art. Did the fact of having taught in the United States validate you in some way when you returned to teach in England?

K F   I don't think that the British were in any way impressed by my experience in the States. After Princeton I came to Columbia in 1972 and stayed until 1974, and then I returned to England from 1974 to 1977, during which time I taught at the Royal College of Art. I had this arrangement with my colleague John Miller that, given that we had both applied for the professorship at the Royal College of Art, whoever got the job would hire the other as a tutor. So John got the professorship and I was hired as a tutor. I went back to London with the idea of repatriating myself definitively.

D T   I understand that at some point you were shortlisted to become the chair of the Architectural Association.   155

K F   Yes, this was around 1971. I was a candidate and the other candidate was Alvin Boyarsky—who was eventually appointed. There was a vote of the school community and I lost it. I should mention that I was backed by Rem Koolhaas and Elia Zenghelis, while Boyarsky was backed by Peter Cook. My pitch was too political, that is Marxist … which was not a very shrewd strategy. It was counterproductive. Boyarsky had taught in Chicago where he had been the associate dean at the Illinois School of Architecture at the University of Illinois. I must say that, in the event, he made a very good chairman of the Architectural Association. He was unbelievably dedicated; he did not do anything else but run the school. And in this regard, he was brilliant. When I look back, they probably chose the right person.

D T How did losing that vote affect you?

K F At different times I tried to repatriate myself. On another occasion, I was a candidate for the professorship of architecture at the University of Cambridge, and I did not get that either. At that time there were three candidates and none of us were appointed to the position. One was Manuel de Solà-Morales, and the other was the County Architect of Hampshire, Colin Stansfield-Smith, someone with a lot of professional experience. They elected someone in-house instead.

D T When did you build the connection with Columbia University? Was it through the IAUS?

K F What had happened was that I had tried to shift from Princeton to Columbia before when Romaldo Giurgola was chairman, but I only achieved the move when James Stewart Polshek became the dean of the school in 1972.

D T When exactly did you arrive at the IAUS in New York?

K F I became a fellow in 1972, parallel to my joining the faculty at Columbia. I then took a leave of absence from Columbia from 1974 to 1977 and taught at the Royal College of Art in London. Before leaving in 1974, I had already been appointed to a full professorship at Columbia.

D T Once established in the United States you did many visiting professorships—the ETH in Zurich, the Berlage Institute in Amsterdam, and the Accademia di Architettura in Mendrisio, for instance. How did all of these transatlantic back-and-forths impact you?

K F I only had one serious contact at the ETH, someone named Franz Oswald. He had studied and taught at Cornell, and afterward he went back to Switzerland and taught in Zurich. He invited me to the ETH as a visiting professor for one semester. My long association with the Berlage Institute came about because of my contact with Herman Hertzberger, who founded the Berlage in 1990 in the famous orphanage designed by Aldo van Eyck. It was a new institution and he wanted me to be part of it. I would, indeed, be involved for seven years, on and off. Then came the professorship in Mendrisio. Although the Berlage was very stimulating, the richer experience was the one in Mendrisio, which was truly crucial because it increased my contact with Italy.

I had written on Mario Botta in 1978 in *Oppositions* and I had been interested in his early work. Also, on an earlier occasion I had met Aurelio Galfetti, so we knew each other. The story, however, with Mendrisio goes back to someone with whom I had worked at Douglas Stephen & Partners: Panos Koulermos. He was a Greek Cypriot who had studied in London with Stephen and then worked for him. Koulermos was married to an Italian woman and he would eventually go to Milan and then, in 1965, to Athens where he established a partnership with Spyros Amourgis and Nikos Kalogeras; they would be an important office for some ten years. Then Panos was invited by Boyarsky to Chicago, and to the University of Southern California where he would briefly serve as the dean of the school of architecture. Panos started to teach at Mendrisio a little bit before me. However, he was permanently in residence, whereas I had a visiting relationship to the school; I would go eight times a year, each time for a week. The only way that this was possible while still maintaining my position at Columbia was because the European and the American university year are slipped in relation to each other. The Europeans do not start until the beginning of October and they go on until July, and the Americans start in September and finish by the end of April, and those shifts enabled me to teach in both places and only have to do one makeup session each semester. That was a very rich experience because it exposed me to a lot of different work and to a different way of thinking.

February 1, 2013

D T   Daniel Talesnik
K F   Kenneth Frampton

D T You once mentioned to me that you think technology in Anglo-American culture has an aura of being "ipso facto progressive," that this is something to be said about Britain and the United States. Which buildings represented this?

K F The Centre Pompidou was surely an Archigram project in the end, or more precisely, a synthesis between Price and Archigram. The idea of a building as a space-frame box was already implicit in Price's Fun Palace. A certain technological euphoria is evident in the Centre Pompidou, with all those colored service pipes up one side of the building and the escalator access tubes on the other. The whole building is conceived as a kind of machine, with human material being fed in on one side and power being fed in or evacuated on the other.

D T Besides the references in your *Modern Architecture: A Critical History*, did you ever write about the Pompidou?

K F Alan Colquhoun wrote brilliantly about the Pompidou, but I did not. I avoided it in a way. I still find it to be a very interesting project, symptomatic of a certain moment. However, it is important to acknowledge that the Pompidou is neither Russian Constructivism, nor is it constructivist in the Hannes Meyer and Hans Wittwer sense. Of course, technology is also present in their work, but it is not rhetorical to the same degree. Even Renzo Piano has acknowledged in hindsight the crudeness of his and Richard Rogers's position on the Pompidou.

D T The connection between the ADGB Trade Union School in Bernau by Meyer and Wittwer and the Hunstanton School in Norfolk by the Smithsons would appear to be more evident.

161

K F I think that the Smithsons' 1953 project for Sheffield University is closer to Meyer and Wittwer's ADGB Bernau school, and that Hunstanton is closer to Mies. [Figs. 44–45] It is not pure Mies, but it is definitely closer to his post-Second World War language. In relation to Hunstanton, the sensibility of brutalism displayed a certain technological rhetoric; the idea that the plumbing system should be revealed, in much the same way as the precast-concrete floor planks are evident as they slot into the steel frame, directly expressed without a suspended ceiling. This was not Mies's position at all. It is fascinating that Price would be close to Mies, with his famous phrase of "well-serviced anonymity." This "Pricean" notion was closer to Mies than either Archigram or the Smithson's Hunstanton.

D T   Since we are mapping out a territory here, how do you see James Stirling in relation to the progressiveness of technology?

K F   What makes brutalism fascinating and difficult to write about is that there was a series of overlapping strands from the beginning. One could say that the Smithsons and Stirling had a moment in common that came with their interest in British brick vernacular, and that continued in Stirling's work up to his 1970 project for Derby Civic Centre (an unbuilt work, designed with Leon Krier). [Fig. 46] Stirling's brick period, so to speak, has been documented in Alan Berman's *Jim Stirling and the Red Trilogy* (2010), and the buildings are the Leicester University Engineering Building (1960–1963), History Faculty, Cambridge (1963–1967), and the Florey Building, Oxford, (1966–1971), all of which show a use of brick as the quintessentially British element. The Smithsons also share this to some extent in the early fifties with their project for the unbuilt Soho House. You could say that Stirling's language became suspended between the technological efficiency of curtain-wall construction and the counter principle of brick-masonry fabric, and you can see these two languages juxtaposed expressively in an empirical way in the Leicester Engineering Building. [Figs. 35–36 on pages 140–141]

D T   So the British High-Tech architects were united by a rejection of the British brick tradition?

K F   Between 1945 and 1960, everyday British life was still, in effect, a preconsumerist society, which was not optimum from the point of view of capitalism. Archigram aspired to a fantasized American utopia, which Price did not indulge in. This British brick obsession was preconsumerist, a kind of ethical poverty, if one could call it that. High-Tech, on the other hand, shared with Archigram an aspiration toward a universal technology, which was redemptive in itself and hence also popular. This came close to the idea of pop art, of course, and was also connected to some extent to brutalism.

This is the popular aspect of brutalism, particularly in the case of the Smithsons and Eduardo Paolozzi; hence their essay "But Today We Collect Ads."[1]

1   Alison Smithson and Peter Smithson, "But Today We Collect Ads," *Architecture d'aujourd'hui* 344 (January 2003): 40–45.

Fig. 44   Hannes Meyer and Hans Wittwer, ADGB Trade Union School, Bernau bei Berlin, Germany, 1928–1930.
              Photograph by Walter Peterhans. Courtesy of Bauhaus-Universität Weimar, Archiv der Moderne.

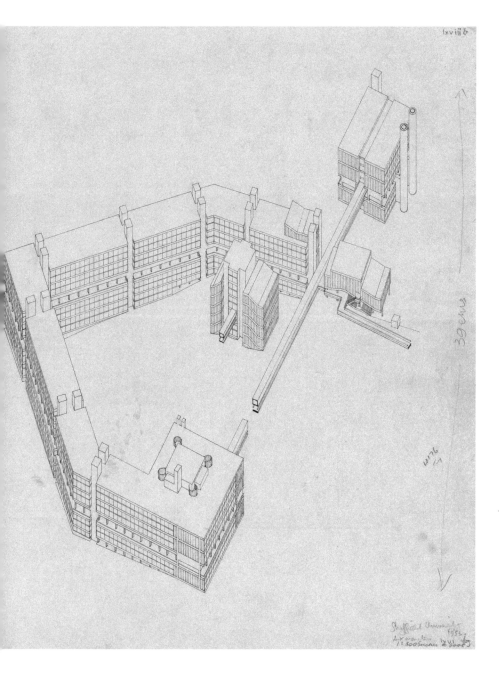

167

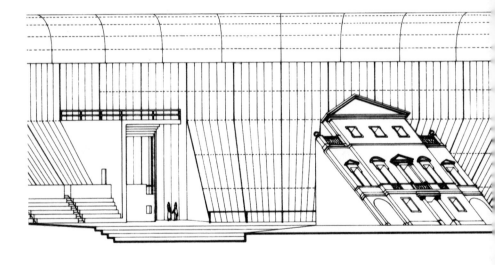

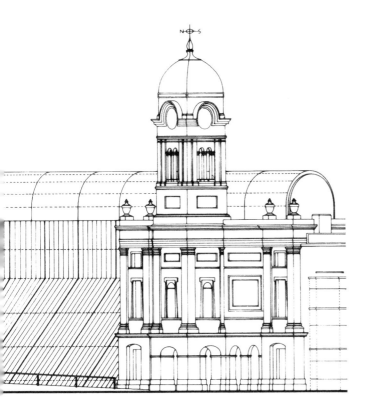

169

October 22, 2013

D T   Daniel Talesnik
K F   Kenneth Frampton

D T   What should the role of an architectural historian be?

K F   Architectural history, like all history, should seek to reveal the cultural pattern of the present and the times that preceded it. This particularly applies to the modern movement and the modern predicament in general. Before 1750, there was no history in the modern sense, so relatively speaking, history was a latecomer compared to literature or law. The historian's role should be interpretative, where the past is always being reworked in the light of the present. I subscribe to E.H. Carr's view as set forth in his book *What is History?*: each age writes its own history so that in this sense there is no absolute history.[1]

D T   How would you describe your project as an architectural historian?

K F   What I have been very loath, in a way, to acknowledge is the fact that I am not, strictly speaking, an architectural historian. When *Labour, Work and Architecture* was published, the essays were grouped under three headings: *theory*, *history*, and *criticism*. In the preface to the book, I try to make the case that I'm not truly speaking either as a theorist or a historian, and not even as a critic on a regular basis. I settled for a "writer on architecture," but I realize this is lame beyond belief. As far as I'm concerned, the first task of the architectural historian is to reinterpret the history of the modern movement. This movement began in real earnest after the First World War, when it was at its highest energy, and came to an end after twenty years with the Spanish Civil War, and with the equally brutal denouement of the Second World War.

The second task is to develop a critical contemporary discourse as I attempted to do in my *Studies in Tectonic Culture: The Poetics of Construction in Nineteenth and Twentieth Century Architecture* (1995). [Fig. 47] This is perhaps a categorical example, in as much as it is a reinterpretation of historical fragments going back to the nineteenth century, a species of operative criticism done in order to afford a ground for architectural practice in the present. *Studies in Tectonic Culture* arose out of my theory of critical regionalism. This concept of critical regionalism was coined in 1981 by Alexander Tzonis and Liliane Lefaivre. In 1983 I wrote "Towards a

Critical Regionalism: Six Points for an Architecture of Resistance," and among these points there is one that raises an implicit opposition between the tectonic and the scenographic, and out of this there finally came *Studies in Tectonic Culture*.

D T Anthony Vidler, in his 2008 book, *Histories of the Immediate Present: Inventing Architectural Modernism*, analyzes the historical periods in which his four case studies located the seeds of modernism. For Emil Kaufmann it was in the neoclassical period, for Colin Rowe it was in mannerism, for Reyner Banham it was in Futurism, and for Manfredo Tafuri it was in the Renaissance. Where do you see the early kernels of the modern project? Do you agree with any of the four historians Vidler talks about?

K F I think that these are examples of protohistories of the modern movement, but what interests me more is the full force of the modern movement after the First World War. That is, from the point of view of models of practice—what happened in Russia, Germany, and the Netherlands after the war is most interesting. It seems to me that the modern movement becomes more finely articulated between the First and Second World Wars. To this must be added the syntactical and semantic articulation achieved by Frank Lloyd Wright, but this is also relatively late compared to the models that Anthony Vidler cites. By 1910, Wright had developed an extraordinarily rich architectural syntax. So those figures are for me more important than the protomoderns that Vidler's case studies appear to be involved with.

D T From *Modern Architecture* to your essay "Towards a Critical Regionalism," and moving forward to *Studies in Tectonic Culture*, what do you think has remained constant in your interests as a historian and what has changed? Do you see your body of work as part of the same narrative?

K F Compared to my early involvement with avant-garde expression in Russia, Germany, and the Netherlands, I suppose I have become more conscious of the poetic potential arising out of structure and modes of construction. I think that what one may detect in *Studies in Tectonic Culture* is a move away from avant-garde aesthetics to a more tectonic discourse based on structure, construction, and material. This has changed in my work. What has remained constant is a commitment to the Socialist aspect of the modern project.

D T   If one reads your articles and books from the sixties until the present, it seems that at the beginning of your career you saw Le Corbusier as the most "revolutionary" architect of the twentieth century, the most accomplished, if you will. However, now I believe you would say that Alvar Aalto is the most relevant modern architect for contemporary practice.

K F   Aalto is the one figure from the so-called "heroic core" of the modern movement active before the Second World War whose legacy is still ripe for further development. [Fig. 48] I think Le Corbusier's semantic is not really available today, largely because the utopian project of the modern movement has been totally foreclosed. Aalto was always measured in his approach with respect to the utopianism of the modern movement; he was always very circumspect about the possibility and/or desirability of realizing a utopian project. The emphasis in Aalto's work on the phenomenological experience of the environment has everything to do with human perception and the human nervous system. This side of his work is still very pertinent and critical, and thus, still very open.

D T   In a previous answer you mentioned that your book *Studies in Tectonic Culture* could be evaluated as a species of "operative criticism," a category used by Manfredo Tafuri to describe aspects of the work of historians like Nikolaus Pevsner, Sigfried Giedion, Bruno Zevi, and Reyner Banham that were intended to guide design practice. Can you elaborate more on your thoughts on operative criticism?

K F   Obviously, I have indulged in the self-same operative criticism; I think this is not inconsistent with my conception of history. I have never concealed the fact that I consider myself to be an operative critic. In that sense, I am limited as a historian because I am too subjective, although I don't think there is such a thing as an objective history.

D   T   How do you think your project as a historian has and/or will affect the discipline?

K   F   It is hard to say. I was recently speaking about architects whose work began with a precise, phenomenological approach and then, at a certain point, became incredibly repetitive and schematic—architects who are competent professionally, but the actual detailing of their work and also its formal patterning has become a kind of easy permutation. Perhaps the digital, apart from the phenomenon of the parametric, has had a profound impact on architectural practice, for the way it encourages a kind of superficial pattern making, either in terms of the figure-ground movement of the plan, or in terms of the surface of the building. If you look at contemporary magazines, you will see one project after another—iterations of the same domino-like distribution of pierced windows across a surface—as if that were sufficient to carry the culture of architecture forward. In my opinion, this aesthetically reductive approach arises out of the facility of digital pattern making. In such work, the plan and the character of the space it contains are no longer seminal. Maybe my greatest impact has been and will be on smaller work. Perhaps we could describe it as an architecture of resistance, but it can be found all over the place. You can find it everywhere but it tends not to be evident at a large scale. It is as though large scale in itself, plus the digital, precludes this kind of refinement and articulation. This comes across when one looks at all the new high-rise buildings being built in New York City; each one is successively more meaningless than the next.

176

1   E. H. Carr, *What is History?*
(New York: Vintage, 1967).

178

181

Colophon

Columbia Books on
Architecture and the City
An imprint of the Graduate
School of Architecture, Planning,
and Preservation

Columbia University
1172 Amsterdam Ave
415 Avery Hall
New York, NY 10027
arch.columbia.edu/books

Distributed by
Columbia University Press
cup.columbia.edu

*Kenneth Frampton: Conversations
with Daniel Talesnik*

Contributors
Kenneth Frampton
Daniel Talesnik
Mary McLeod

ISBN
978 1 941332 64 1

Library of Congress Control Number
2022952362

Copy Editor
Catherine Bindman

Graphic Designer
Scott Vander Zee

Lithographer
Marjeta Morinc

Printer
DZA Druckerei zu Altenburg GmbH

Paper
Lessebo Smooth White 240 g/m²
Lessebo Smooth White 100 g/m²

Typeface
BT Grotesk Regular
BT Grotesk Italic

Director of Publications
Isabelle Kirkham-Lewitt

Assistant Director
Joanna Joseph

Assistant Editor
Meriam M. Soltan